A COMMUNITY
of DISCIPLES

Making your parish all it can be

DES ROBERTSON

NEW LONDON, CT 06320
WWW.23RDPUBLICATIONS.COM

TWENTY-THIRD PUBLICATIONS
A Division of Bayard
One Montauk Avenue, Suite 200
New London, CT 06320
(860) 437-3012 or (800) 321-0411
www.23rdpublications.com

Library of Congress Cataloging-in-Publication Data

Robertson, Des.
  A community of disciples : making your parish all it can be / Des Robertson.
     p. cm.
  Includes bibliographical references.
  ISBN 978-1-58595-857-3
  1. Church. 2. Church attendance. 3. Discipling (Christianity) 4. Catholic Church—Doctrines. I. Title.
  BX1746.R625 2012
  253.088'282—dc23
                          2012016572

Cover image by Elizabeth Wang, Copyright ©2011 Radiant Light, Image code R-60034-CW, www.radiantlight.org.uk

Printed in the U.S.A.

To my wife, Debbie
who, by her example,
has taught me so much about the
meaning of unconditional love

I give you a new commandment: love one another. As I have loved you, so you also should love one another. This is how all will know that you are my disciples, if you have love for one another.

JOHN 13:34–35

CONTENTS

PREFACE

L et's face it: We can no longer kid ourselves that the problem will go away if we just ignore it. It is widely acknowledged that the Church is struggling to proclaim the good news in the affluent West—Europe, North America, and Australia. While there may be many baptized Christians, the numbers of those who are obviously and actively practicing their faith are declining each year. There are fewer people in the pews, and while many people claim that they do things because they are Christian, they are not necessarily doing these things to give witness to Christ. Often people are reluctant to talk about their faith to others, even when they are asked, because our secular society would have us believe that it is not politically correct to do so. As a result, good deeds alone can be too easily interpreted as an act of kindness and left at that. They do not necessarily point people to the kingdom.

It is too easy to blame the decline on the scandals, as horrific as they are, compounded by the bad handling of the issue by the hierarchy. No doubt the scandals and the way they were handled have had a significant impact, but the issue is much more complex than that.

The real issue is that society in the affluent West is freer than it has ever been. It is this freedom that has not allowed the scandals to be swept under the carpet. It is this freedom that calls for a more mature Church that is willing to help people to find the answers they are searching for, rather than to present answers to questions that most people are not asking.

To suggest that the liberal approach following Vatican II has caused the problem is wishful thinking by those who mourn the loss of the time when the authority of the hierarchy in the Church was not easily questioned. In my view the pace of decline of the Church in the West would have been significantly greater had we not had Vatican II. I doubt whether the Church would be growing as it is in the Third World had we not had Vatican II.

I know this is an oversimplification, but for me, Vatican II chose love instead of fear as the way forward. That makes an awful lot of sense when we believe in a God who is Love. The Holy Spirit pointed the way, and we have to have the courage to follow that path. It is not possible to bring about a change on the scale of Vatican II across a population of more than a billion Catholics in a mere fifty years. This is especially true when the council only provided the framework, with little detail of how to bring it to life. We were given the direction but we can only find the way by embarking on the journey. Change happens across a community only after each person in that community changes their heart and mind. This is especially true when the change affects anything related to our values, and faith is right at the core of our values.

Of course, some people misunderstand or misinterpret the intentions of Vatican II and run off to do weird and wonderful things. Mistakes have been and will be made, but that does not mean that Vatican II was wrong or that we should backtrack. Each mistake is just a signpost pointing to something that will break down rather than build up Christ's Church. We should learn from those wrong turns and get back on track. We are just scratching the surface in terms of understanding Vatican II in order to implement it. There is a long journey ahead of us, and we need courageous and visionary leaders to guide us on that journey. It is not a job for the faint-hearted.

This book is about helping ordinary people, together with ever fewer parish priests—the ordinary day-to-day body of Christ—to build up Christ's Church in practical ways in our parishes. It is not easy to do this, but every job becomes easier when you know why you are doing it and understand why things happen as they do. People don't behave as they did one hundred, fifty, or even twenty years ago. Expecting them to behave as their parents and grandparents did is not going to work. If we make an effort to understand why they behave as they do, we may find better ways of being more relevant as a Church. When you know what to expect it is much easier to know what you have to do to get the job done.

This book attempts to explain some of the issues facing today's Church, and also takes a possibly uncomfortable look at why we are not as effective as we could be. I freely acknowledge that my interpretation may not reflect the whole story and that others may interpret things differently. I don't have all the answers, and I will be more than delighted if this book just stimulates conversations in the Church about finding a more effective way in which to "make disciples of all nations." I can only speak from my experience. I have lived in Southern Africa and the UK, and I have also researched parish development in Australia and the USA. I have seen some amazing parishes thriving in both poor and affluent communities. It is a fallacy to suggest that people only turn to God when they have few material possessions, although God obviously may be more attractive to the poor.

It may help to think of this as a guide for the journey and not a map. There is no single way of getting there. But certain practices have proven to be effective irrespective of any way of organizing or of cultural differences, and I offer these ideas for consideration.

Before we jump straight into practical things that can be done to become a more effective Church, we need to recognize that not everyone shares the same vision of what Church is, or even what our purpose is on this planet. We cannot expect to work together without a common purpose or a common understanding of what it is we are intended to be.

I start the book by considering what our purpose is. I then offer a model of Church that I hope is inclusive and can be accepted by all who genuinely believe that the Church is intended to be one, holy, universal, and apostolic. After that I suggest practical ways in which we can be that Church more effectively, with ideas on how to start in even the smallest, most humble community, with little or no money.

There are chapters on how to sustain and grow this way of being Church. I also look at some of the issues that may create barriers to our effectiveness, and our frequent emphasis on moral theology at the expense of a pastoral theology. Rather than simply offering criticisms, I hope to raise questions to make us all think, in the hope of finding a better way.

For some this book may be challenging. I hope that these people will step back from their fears and recognize that we cannot continue as we are. In suggesting that some of our practices are not as they should be, my intention is only to strive to find a better way to build up Christ's Church. There is no point in burying our heads in the sand and simply working harder. Working ever harder at doing the same things is not going to produce a different result. It's only going to accelerate the pace of decline as those who are already working hard become ever more stressed and so unable to do any work at all.

I am not promoting some kind of new movement or five-year program. This is not some kind of silver bullet that will provide a quick fix. This approach is no more or less than a framework to help everyone do what Christ called them to do: become his disciples so we can be more effective as the Church we are intended to be. In all that we do, it's important to remember that the Church is God's gift to us. We have to accept our responsibility to proclaim the good news and build up the Church.

Embark on this journey at your own pace, but always expect, empower, and support the people around you to be disciples of Christ. Do what you can now, even if it is not much, but know where you are going and why. Keep building on what you have already done and the new things you do using what you learn in this book. Don't turn back when you hit obstacles, and soon you will find that each year when you evaluate progress at the Triduum, the Church in your parish will be stronger, more faithful, and growing steadily.

In every successful parish, the pastor is clearly the leader of the parish and is both loved and respected by the parishioners. The parishioners are not just actively encouraged to use their gifts and talents to build up the Church; *they are expected to do so*. The pastor willingly delegates responsibility but does so appropriately, ensuring that the people are always able to perform their required role. Ongoing lifelong formation is always a critical success factor, to a point where some successful parishes claim formation as their charism.

While the pastor sets high standards, he does not expect perfection and knows things will go wrong from time to time. When they do, he mostly smiles (even if he is gritting his teeth), and he supports those involved in picking up the pieces and trying again. There is always a clear recognition, indeed celebration, that despite our imperfections, we are all of us—clergy, religious, and laity—called to accept co-responsibility for the life and mission of the Church.

We do this best as a community of disciples, worshiping, learning, and working to live and share a life in Christ.

ONE

Our mission

We are a missionary Church. Do we understand what this means? Before going further, it may be a good idea to stop a moment and consider what our mission is, before we set out to achieve it. The starting point obviously has to be with God. No doubt the end point should be as well—the Alpha and the Omega.

Scripture and the Church guide us to understand God and our relationship with him, but sometimes we tend to overcomplicate things. This is not surprising because God is both infinitely complex and infinitely simple. A couple of verses from Scripture sum up our best understanding of God, our relationship with him, and what is expected of us:

> God is love, and whoever remains in love remains in God and God in him. In this is love brought to perfection among us, that we have confidence on the day of judgment because as he is, so are we in this world. There is no fear in love, but perfect love drives out fear because fear has to do with punishment, and so one who fears is not yet perfect in love. 1 JOHN 4:16-18

If we want to become one with God, then we need to strive to become love as God is love. It makes sense—if we are not love, then we are not compatible with love, and we cannot be compatible with God.

God is love. But this is a vast oversimplification. God is within, above, and beyond love and infinitely beyond that again, way beyond anything we can grasp. And so, it is true to state that God is love—but not as we understand love. God's love is beyond perfection or any of the other limits we may place on it. But because we need to be practical and rely on our own best but inadequate human understanding of God, let's accept that God is love. I feel certain that a loving God does not want us to complicate it any more than that. God will be more than happy if we strive to become love in our best inadequate way, so we can be one with him.

We cannot hope to understand God but, in our natural desire to be one with him, we are driven to try to understand. And as we seek to understand, ever more is revealed to us. In exploring my relationship with God and Church, the simple understanding "God is love" is always my point of departure. When I hear confusing or contradictory messages, I always come back to this truth to start my questioning and discernment.

If God is love, then our understanding of love will help us to explore and better understand God. So what do we know about love?

We know that you can't do love alone, and this immediately raises the question: How could God be love before creation, if he had no one to love? Suddenly the Trinity makes sense. In the Trinity, God is a relationship of three in one, a perfect relationship of love.

If God is already in a perfect relationship of love, in need of nothing, why did God make us? After all, he is an Almighty God, the source of all power and love. There is nothing and no one greater. Nothing exists outside of his creation. He has nothing to fear and needs nothing from anyone or anything because everything is from him. What else could he possibly need? Why bother to make us?

One of the strange things about love is that it never runs out. The more you love, the more love you have to give. Love is creative and life-giving. This makes sense when we think about God. There is no limit to God and so love has no limits, because love is God.

And in this we have the answer as to why God made us: He made us just to love us, because that's what God does!

God does not need us to love him or serve him. He is the great big God, the source of all. God needs nothing. His love is not conditional upon our good behavior or good deeds. We cannot earn God's love. It is a free, unconditional gift, because his love is beyond perfect.

And so the first aspect of our relationship with God is that he loves us unconditionally. Love always involves self-giving, and so God makes no demands on us. Perfect love is perfectly generous, and God takes self-giving to the extreme. God wants to give us all that he has and is. He offers us the ultimate gift of being one with him.

This is the next key aspect of our understanding. Our relationship with God, indeed our very existence, is not limited to the space and time of our life on Earth. God desires that we become one with him for all eternity. Death is simply a milestone in the journey of our relationship with God. Death is nothing to be feared, and the end of life on this planet is not a bad thing.

A gift, even such a great gift as being one with God for all eternity, is no gift unless we are free to accept it or reject it. It would have no meaning if we had no power to choose a different way of life to the one God desires for us. And so God surrenders his power over us and gives us a free will to use all the power he has given us in any way we choose. We can even try to use that power against him, if we want. In a strange way, our ability to do evil is proof of God's unconditional love for us!

And that begs the question: How can God allow innocent people to be harmed by the evil acts of others? It is true that our bodies can be hurt and even destroyed by others, but our life is not harmed or destroyed. As I said earlier, death on this planet is just a milestone on our journey to eternal life in God, who just wants to love us. Nothing can harm our spirit except we ourselves. The only way we can harm our eternal spirit of life is to refuse to love. Sin is no more or less than a refusal to love.

And so, another aspect of our relationship with God is being completely free to choose how to use the power God has given us.

Because all is from God, God is in all. He is in us, closer than our own heartbeat, around us, above us, and beyond us. Again this makes sense. Another characteristic of love is a desire for closeness with the object of your love. God, being all-capable, is closer than anything we can imagine.

The fact that we can never fully understand God does not stop us from trying, nor should it. It is part of our search for meaning and purpose. Our life is a journey of discovery, and if God is the great creator, then all discoveries inexorably lead us better to understand God. Some may fear science, but good, solid, objective science is the friend of faith because God stands up to scrutiny.

So what understanding can we gain from this very brief analysis in terms of our relationship with God, our faith, Church, and the meaning and purpose of our lives?

If God is a relationship of creative love and we are to become one with God, then by implication we do not do this alone. To be

God-like we should strive to be in a creative relationship of love. I don't believe we can say, "I am created in the image and likeness of God," because a single individual cannot and does not reflect a relationship of love. You can't do love alone. We are intended to be in a loving, creative relationship with God and one another:

> God created man in his image; in the divine image he created him; male and female he created them. God blessed them, saying to them: "Be fertile and multiply..."
>
> GENESIS 1:27-28

The family is the obvious primary model of this relationship of love, but it is not exclusive. The Church is intended to reflect the image and likeness of God as a life-giving, creative community of love. We are the family of God. We are intended to be a community of loving relationships with God and one another: "Thus, the Church has been seen as 'a people made one with the unity of the Father, the Son and the Holy Spirit'" (*Lumen Gentium*, #4).

Is it possible to have a relationship with God and exclude my neighbor, when God is in my neighbor? Surely we cannot have a relationship with selected parts of God? We cannot love God unless we love our neighbor.

> No one has ever seen God. Yet, if we love one another, God remains in us, and his love is brought to perfection in us. This is how we know that we remain in him and he in us, that he has given us of his Spirit.   1 JOHN 4:12-13

Who is our neighbor? If God made us individually different in detail from others, he must love diversity. Who are we to object to what God has created? God is a great and loving God. He does not make rubbish. It's no big deal to accept anyone who is different from us. Nor do we accept those who are different as objects of our piety. They are simply our brothers and sisters. No one is to be excluded from our community of the Church—God's family.

The Church, the people of God in the body of Christ as the temple of the Holy Spirit, is intended to be a life-affirming, creative relationship of love, drawing in, building up, and serving all of God's creation, just as God does.

Our life on earth is about choice. How are we going to choose to use the power God has given us? Will we cling to that power, trying to gain advantage over others for fear that we may become vulnerable to abuse from them, or will we choose to overcome fear and release ourselves from the power others have over us through unconditional forgiveness by practicing love?

This life is not about preparing for a life hereafter about which we have little knowledge. Our life now should be lived to the full, learning to experience the joy Christ promised us when we share the love of God with others. We truly can experience the kingdom of God at every stage of our journey to eternal unity with God.

Love is not an intellectual choice. You experience love by living it. We live it by giving it away. As a sacramental church we become the sacrament, the outward sign of God's gift of his love to us, when we pass that love on to others. When we try to hold onto God's love and keep it to our self, it loses its effectiveness. We smother it and we fail to benefit from that love. When we pass that love on by sharing it with others, God showers more love on us, more than we can ever hope to pass on, and we become a channel of his love for others. We become the sacrament.

Saying it like this, it sounds so easy. Anyone who has tried unconditional love knows how fear always seems to get in the way. All we can hope to do is to try our best. When it is hard to love, our best approach is to act as if we do, even if we feel insincere and we don't live it in our hearts. Our poorest efforts are always magnified by God's generosity, and the more we act as if we love, the more real it will become. Faith is not something abstract focusing on core beliefs. Faith is a lived relationship with God and all of his creation.

So what is our mission, our purpose, once we have chosen love over fear and become a member of the Church? To approach the day of judgment fearlessly, we need to become as God is—Love.

> In this is love brought to perfection among us, that we have confidence on the day of judgment because as he is, so are we in this world.   1 JOHN 4:17

The purpose of our lives is to strive to become love, as God is love, so that we can become one with God. That's it. No more—no less.

TWO

Why is the Church
so often seen as irrelevant?

I f my claim that loving as God loves is the life and mission of the Church, how come the Church is seen as irrelevant by so many in our Western society today? Surely everyone wants to love and be loved, accepted, and cared about?

Before I go any further, it must be acknowledged that there are many wonderful, alive, and active parishes to which my criticisms clearly do not apply. And like most successful organizations, they are unlikely to be afraid of stepping back from time to time to see if there is room for improvement, or if complacency may be creeping in to undermine the wonderful work they are doing.

Hardly anybody enjoys taking a good hard look at what is not working well. The analysis that follows is not intended to point fingers at anyone. It is simply my view based on my experience. We need to search out the light of Christ and follow it. Unless and until the Church is growing and the gospel is being effectively proclaimed wherever we are, we cannot expect to build up the Church without examining and questioning our current practices.

From what I see about me and from what I know of those parts of the world where I have lived, most of our parishes preach a message that exhorts us to *go out*: "What you do to the least of my brethren…" and "Love one another as I have loved you…" and "Go and make disciples of all nations…"

But in practice too many of us *remain in*. We receive the Holy Eucharist. Some of us confess our sins periodically. We say our prayers. We strive to keep the commandments. Not only do many of us not go out, we don't form community with those within. Year in and year out we sit in the same pews and don't know the names of people who attend the same Mass with us, week after week, year after year.

We are not in some new dark age. Humanity has always struggled with living the message of God. Vatican II reminds us: "In the present age, too, it does not escape the Church how great a distance lies between the message she offers and the human failings of those to whom the Gospel is entrusted" (*Gaudium et Spes*, #43).

For many Catholics, the Holy Eucharist is only seen as the *summit* of our faith. After all, what more could there be than to receive the Body and Blood of Our Lord Jesus Christ? The fact that it is also the *source* is mostly forgotten. Seekers follow the Rite of Christian Initiation of Adults (RCIA) process, building close, trusting relationships with others as they explore their faith. But after Easter, when they are welcomed into the Church, they drop into a void. The message we seem to give is: "Now that you are one of us, you may receive the Holy Eucharist with the rest of us. That's it. What more could you want?"

Why is it that so many people received into the Church at Easter are not attending Mass a year later? Do they perhaps have an expectation of being able to use their gifts and talents to serve Christ incarnate in the neighbor, continuing their growth in learning and faith, forming community, and by their example inspiring others to join the Church? Do we provide these opportunities for all our members?

Jesus did not ask us to worship him. He asked us to follow him.

In many parishes the model of Church is centered almost exclusively around the Holy Eucharist. As a result, if someone is unable to receive the Holy Eucharist for whatever reason, they are effectively excluded from the Church. Little else is offered to people on their journey to the kingdom.

Has faith been ritualized to a point where purpose and meaning have been lost? Have we lost sight of the fact that our whole life is a journey to the kingdom, in which we have to grow and mature in our life in Christ? Is faith really just about qualifying to receive the sacraments? Do our rituals dictate that we receive different sacraments at predefined stages in our lives irrespective of whether we are ready or not?

Faith is a gift of the Holy Spirit. Surely there must be a place in the Church for everyone on that pilgrimage to the kingdom, even when that gift has not yet been received and, yes, even when they are unable to receive the sacraments! They may not be in communion to receive the sacraments, but there is ample evidence that God is happy to use anyone to pass on his message of love. In allowing those not in a state of grace to serve others, might they not grow closer to God and desire to live a different life in Christ? When we only offer the Holy Eucharist in our model of Church, we exclude all the others who may be struggling to find their way on the journey to the kingdom. This is not the example Jesus gave us: "The Pharisees and scribes began to complain, saying, 'This man welcomes sinners and eats with them'" (Luke 15:2).

On our journey to the kingdom, we are expected to grow in our understanding of God and our relationship with him. We are expected to mature in our faith. We cannot do this without some form of guidance or ongoing formation throughout our lives. A ten-minute homily on a Sunday is not enough to meet this need.

In a world where, for many, science threatens faith, where people expect to be able to question and need to be convinced, it is not enough simply to state dogma and doctrine without reasoned explanation. In that approach, people only hear what they cannot do. Where is the attraction of God's love in that?

This is still a holdover from the time when the laity was actively discouraged from questioning and debate. I regularly come across people who view questioning as a lack of faith. But faith is not blind acceptance of doctrine and dogma. Faith is an acceptance of the reality of our Divine Creator who made us just to love us. In that acceptance there is a desire to know him. When you cannot directly see, hear, and touch what you seek to understand, it helps to study the evidence of God. We find that evidence in his creation, especially in our relationships with one another. Through love we come to experience God, because God is the love in our relationships. If our model of Church emphasizes a relationship between God and me and not communion between God and us together, it will be very difficult to find God, because we exclude relationships with each other where God is present in our love.

In many parishes we still suffer from a style of leadership that may have worked in a different time, but today it inhibits our ability to answer Christ's call to the apostolate. In 1906, Pope Pius X stated:

> It follows that the Church is essentially an unequal society, that is, a society comprising two categories of persons, the Pastors and the flock, those who occupy a rank in the different degrees of the hierarchy and the multi-

tude of the faithful. So distinct are these categories that with the pastoral body only rests the necessary right and authority for promoting the end of the society and directing all its members to that end; the one duty of the multitude is to allow themselves to be led, and, like a docile flock, to follow the Pastors.   *VEHEMENTOR NOS, #8*

That authoritarian leadership style sets priests up for failure in the free and educated society of the twenty-first century, where people quietly just empty the pews, leaving their pastors increasingly frustrated by their ineffectiveness. All too often, we see these leaders, formed for a different time, mourning the lack of faith in society today, as they retreat into administering the sacraments, caring for buildings, and concentrating on serving an older generation of Catholics, who still pray, pay, obey, and "help Father."

Contrast Pope Pius X's statement above with Pope Benedict XVI's address to the people of his diocese, Rome, on May 26, 2009, in which he makes it clear that all members are responsible for the being and action of the Church. Here are some extracts to challenge us:

[We should] understand ever better what this Church is, this People of God in the Body of Christ....[We should] improve pastoral structures in such a way that the co-responsibility of all the members of the People of God in their entirety is gradually promoted....[The Laity] must no longer be viewed as "collaborators" of the clergy but truly recognized as "co-responsible," for the Church's being and action, thereby fostering the consolidation of a mature and committed laity....This common awareness of being Church of all the baptized in no way diminishes the responsibility of parish priests. It is precisely your task, dear parish priests, to nurture the spiritual and apostolic growth of those who are already committed to working hard in the parishes. They form the core of the community that will act as a leaven for the others.

For as long as we see the Holy Eucharist only as the ultimate summit and not also the source of our faith, the Church will increasingly be seen as irrelevant.

As long as the Church fails to practice what it preaches in terms of going out to serve Christ incarnate in our neighbor, the Church will increasingly be seen as irrelevant.

As long as we expect no more formation of the faithful than religious education in school and a ten-minute homily at Mass on a Sunday, the Church will increasingly be seen as irrelevant.

As long as we see our faith as a relationship between God and me and exclude communion with our neighbor, the Church will increasingly be seen as irrelevant.

As long as the daily example of our lives as Christians does not inspire others to be fully human as God intended, the Church will increasingly be seen as irrelevant.

As long as members of the laity are expected to be a docile, unquestioning flock, blindly following their pastor, the Church will be seen as irrelevant.

These are strong statements and they beg the questions:
- Why now?
- What has changed?
- Why do things that worked before apparently no longer work?

The short answer is that knowledge has shifted power from the hands of the few to the hands of the masses.

There are three forms of earthly power: might, wealth, and knowledge. Might is the most primitive form of power. If my stick or my gun or my army is bigger than yours, I can force you to carry out my will. Wealth is more powerful than might because wealth can buy sticks and guns and armies and deceit. Knowledge, especially truth, is more powerful than might and wealth, because knowledge of the truth empowers the human spirit and overcomes deceit. When knowledge is easily shared, its power to influence is immeasurable.

Since the invention of the printing press, through books, newspapers, radio, television, computers, and the Internet, knowledge has moved from the few to the masses. Never before have such great numbers of humankind been so well educated. Never before have such numbers been as wealthy as a result of that knowledge. This has led to freedom on a scale not experienced before.

Where previously there was an obvious difference in objectives between capital (those with the wealth) and labor (the masses), this no longer exists. The value in virtually every business now is not in its buildings, plant, and machinery, but in the knowledge in the heads of its employees. As a result, workers are increasingly becoming partners and shareholders in the companies they work for. Power has shifted to the masses.

That power shift has changed politics and, in the western world at least, there are far fewer ideology differences between political parties. The debate is shifting ever more to who will do more about the economy, energy, and ecology.

This shift in power that knowledge has brought about causes people to question and challenge those in authority, whether they be bosses, doctors, politicians, priests, or bishops. No longer can it be expected that people will accept an answer simply because someone in authority gives it. People need to be persuaded of the truth. It has to fit in with their experience to be accepted. It is not enough to say, "It is a mystery. You must have faith," when we are unable to explain the contradictions in our teachings and hypocrisy in our practices. Today we need both faith and reason to proclaim the gospel.

While many may lament "the good old days" when those in authority were obeyed, I submit that the freedom we have today is exactly as God intended. No one can force us to choose God. That choice has to be made freely and willingly and against all other options, in order to be valid. To choose to become love as God is love calls for a surrender of our power back to God. It is no small thing, and nobody else could or should make that choice for us.

> Only in freedom can man direct himself toward goodness....For its part, authentic freedom is an exceptional sign of the divine image within man. For God has willed that man remain "under the control of his own decisions," so that he can seek his Creator spontaneously, and come freely to utter and blissful perfection through loyalty to Him. Hence man's dignity demands that he act according to a knowing and free choice that is personally motivated and prompted from within, not under blind internal impulse, nor by mere external pressure.
>
> GAUDIUM ET SPES, #17

In the past it was much easier to give instructions to be obeyed rather than to reason and persuade. But in a society where our example is the one thing most likely to influence others, we need to be open to be challenged and to have to explain ourselves. Let's face it; we all are much more committed when a choice we make is well considered and free.

■ Individuality and consumerism

Our human rights legislation emphasizes the rights of the individual, often above communal rights. Individual rights are good but when an individual consistently places self above all else, the whole of society suffers. There is no doubt that people today are more concerned with self. The first question anyone seems to ask before agreeing to anything is "What's in it for me?"

We are all consumers. We need to consume in order to survive. Before industrialization we were far more in touch with the production process of what we consumed, and the consequences of our consumption were far more obvious to us. We knew that milk came from cows and not out of a bottle from the supermarket. We were closer to the farmer down the road and could see the effect on his children of refusing to pay him a fair price for his products. We knew how hard he worked to produce our food because we could see him laboring from before dawn into the evening.

Today, what we consume has become a commodity that is divorced from the production process. We see nothing of the value of the work that has gone into producing it. The only thing we value is how good the article looks or functions against the price we pay. The article in the supermarket is divorced from its production process and the people who made it. The proportion of money earned at each stage of the supply chain is irrelevant to us. As a result we are able to consume without feeling any responsibility for the people who have labored to make the item available to us.

Along with our sense of individuality comes our lack of accountability for any aspect of what we consume, other than ensuring that we get good quality for the money we pay. None of us is immune to this. Even the most righteous among us find it hard to resist a bargain in the supermarket.

The Church is not immune to the culture of consumerism. The most common complaint I hear from priests is that so many people have a supermarket approach to the Holy Eucharist. They pop into church on a Sunday to receive and consume the Holy Eucharist for their own benefit.

But when parish priests believe that their prime function is to provide a service, whether this is administering the sacraments, visiting the sick, or preparing people for the sacraments, this reinforces commodification of the practices of our faith for convenient consumption. When the Church decides that children should be lined up in production lines at pre-defined ages to receive the sacraments, the sacraments become a commodity to be consumed at the appointed time. When we consume the Host as a commodity, the Holy Eucharist is divorced from its meaning and purpose. Eucharistic services can also promote the Eucharist as a commodity, making it readily available for our convenient consumption, divorced from its purpose. In such a culture, we come to venerate the building of the church as the place where God is conveniently kept for our consumption, and so we spend far more money on buildings than we spend on caring for the least among us or on proclaiming the gospel.

The prime function of the priest is not to provide services, but to exhort, enable, and support us to live the Eucharistic life, a life in Christ. The call to love one another cannot be outsourced to the priest for our convenience, nor should some priests prevent people from trying to answer their call to the apostolate, as sadly still happens.

> ...by offering the Immaculate Victim, not only through the hands of the priest, but also with him, [the faithful] should learn also to offer themselves; through Christ the

> Mediator, they should be drawn day by day into ever more
> perfect union with God and with each other, so that finally
> God may be all in all.   *SACROSANCTUM CONCILIUM*, #48

The starting point is to recognize that we too are part of that society and culture. We are not intended to live apart from it but rather to live the gospel within it, in contrast to the culture and norms of our society. It does not help to lament the wrongs and feel sorry for ourselves. It is precisely our job to show how a life in Christ can be lived in a joyful, fully human way, just as Jesus showed us.

We need to examine whether in the practice of our faith, we are in fact promoting individualism rather than helping to overcome it. Is the practice of our faith focused on saving our own soul and getting into heaven? Is a focus on not sinning seen as the path to heaven? Is our prayer between God and me? Do we go to Mass for a quiet time with God? Does salvation only mean forgiveness of my sins? If these are the motivations and characteristics of the practice of our faith, then it is a very individualistic faith.

If we want to undermine individualism without compromising the rights of the individual, then the practice of our faith should concentrate on learning to become love as God is love, so we can become one with him and all of his creation. We do this by engaging with and loving our neighbor. If these are our practices, then our motivation goes beyond personal salvation to working to bring about a Holy Communion in the kingdom of God.

> We love because he first loved us. If anyone says, "I love
> God," but hates his brother, he is a liar; for whoever does
> not love a brother whom he has seen cannot love God
> whom he has not seen.   1 JOHN 4:19-20

In this context we remember that the root of the word "salvation" means *to become whole*, which encompasses, but is much more than, simply being forgiven our sins. Becoming whole is all about being one with God and each other in the kingdom—a Holy Communion.

The failure of nerve that, in the face of a free, educated, consumer society, causes so many to attempt to close the windows that were flung so wide open at Vatican II undermines our efforts to be a universal Church, guided by the Holy Spirit and striking out in confidence for the deep waters to fully engage with society. Retreat is not an option if we reject what we see in society. It is precisely because we don't like what we see in society that we have to proclaim the relevance of the gospel confidently, loudly, and clearly within all of society.

This means engaging with people exactly where they are and being prepared to "sell" (explain) the benefits of a life in Christ so they can understand how he relates to them here and now in all the messiness and reality of life and hopefully choose to "buy" (accept) him. Better still, like the apostles, we need to allow them to "try before they buy." Jesus did not require the apostles to believe in order to follow him. They belonged first to discover what he was about. Discipleship is about learning and putting that learning into practice. It is hoped that faith will follow as a gift of the Holy Spirit, as people become receptive to the call through discipleship.

■ Both "where" and "how"

We need a lot more public theological reflection on the world around us. We need to engage with people not just where they are, but also *how* they engage with each other. Local communities are breaking down as people become more mobile, but at the same time social networking is becoming the new way of interacting. I am the first to acknowledge that the breakdown of the local face-to-face community is not a good thing, but if we engage with people where they are (needing contact) and how (online), it becomes possible to start to form the trusted relationships that are necessary in order to share the relevance of the gospel in our lives today. As that relationship grows, it become possible to invite people to become learners and workers for Christ (disciples) and then start building up real community in Holy Communion with God and each other.

Clearly this is not the only form of contact that applies. There are many technologically excluded members of society that we also have to engage with in relevant ways. The point I am making is that we cannot exclude any means of contact simply because it may have a downside. If that's how people interact, that's how we need to engage with them and welcome them to join us on the pilgrimage to the kingdom.

■ Stages of faith

In a free society, we should recognize that faith has different levels of maturity. Throughout their lives, people commonly change and adjust in their faith maturity. As their understanding of their faith changes, so does their approach to practicing their faith. In order to meet people where they are, it may be useful to consider broadly what those stages of faith are, so that we can try to recognize them in the people around us and thereby better understand why they behave as they do. In that way, we can develop ways of interacting with people on their journey of faith that are appropriate and relevant to different stages of faith, thereby promoting mature and active faith practices within the Church. If we expect all people to conform to the behavior of one particular stage of faith, others who are at a different stage of faith will increasingly see the Church as irrelevant.

James Fowler identified seven stages of faith, which clearly are not absolute, but because they make a lot of sense, they are very useful to help us understand why people behave as they do, relative to their faith. His book *Becoming Adult, Becoming Christian* (Fowler, 2000) is a very useful analysis of a key sign of our times.

The stages of faith have nothing whatsoever to do with the depth of faith anyone may have. They simply indicate a level of faith maturity. The faith of a child can easily be stronger than a mature adult, but as that child grows up, their approach to their faith will change even as that faith grows stronger—or perhaps weaker. Paul taught us: "When I was a child, I used to talk as a child, think as a child, reason as a child; when I became a man, I put aside childish things. At present we see indistinctly, as in a mirror, but then face to face. At present I know partially; then I shall know fully, as I am fully known" (1 Cor 13:11–12).

Changes from one stage of faith to another are rarely sudden events, but rather follow as a result of thinking about and exploring our understanding of faith and our values as we mature. It is not the norm to have a clean, orderly progression from one stage to another at periodic intervals on the journey of life. There tends to be a shift rather than a dramatic change from one stage to another, particularly in the later stages. As a result, it is common for people to fluctuate between different stages as they become less of one and more of another. Transitions happen because we come to see ourselves and the world around us differently as the result of a shift in what we know and value. But if people do not question their knowledge and values, there is unlikely to be a stage transition: "Faith stage transitions represent significant alterations in the structures of one's knowing and valuing and, therefore, in the basic orientation and responses of the self" (Fowler, 2000, p 45). (See the Appendix for a fuller analysis of Fowler's Stages of Faith.)

■ Secularity and Judeo-Christianity

It is interesting to consider what Ronald Rolheiser has to say in *Secularity and the Gospel*, in the context of the stages of faith. He suggests that:

> ...secularity is not our enemy, but our child, the child of the Judeo-Christian tradition. But it is not yet full grown, mature enough to fully understand and appreciate what it has drawn from its parents. Too often we see this manifest in a certain adolescent grandiosity, in an arrogant and hostile attitude towards its own roots. However, as is the case with any adolescent child, this is quite understandable, even if unpleasant.   P. 59

> ...its deep structure incarnates many of the moral strengths one finds inside the Judeo-Christian tradition. Sometimes its critics forget that, while secularity mandates freedom from religion, it also mandates freedom for religion, and its moral strengths run deep, even if those moral qualities are no longer attributed by many secularists to any religious source. Simply stated, secular culture, with some inconsistencies notwithstanding, contains much of what is best morally in the Judeo-Christian tradition: human dignity, fundamental honesty, concern for others, democracy, equal voice for everyone, equality of race and gender, equal opportunity for all, tol-

> erance of others and their differences, sexual responsi-
> bility, solutions for conflict that do not involve violence
> and war, hospitality, decency, fairness, and an openness
> to God and the transcendent.
> ...Critics of course are quick to point out that secular
> culture does not always demonstrate these moral quali-
> ties. True, but Christianity does not always demonstrate
> its ideals either.   P. 41

If secularity is indeed the teenage child of Judeo-Christianity, what obligations does it place on us as "parents"? If we are to raise this child to full maturity, at what stage does our faith maturity need to be? As a parent, I know that if I try to place the same restrictions on a twenty-year-old as I would on a ten-year-old, I am not going to get a good reaction.

So where does this leave us?

We cannot expect people to belong to a Church that demands blind adherence to its dogma and doctrine. Nor will they be attracted to a Church that is unquestioning, exclusive, and where the majority of its members do not obviously practice what it preaches.

We cannot expect to drag people who have evolved to a greater understanding of their faith back to a previous level in a free society. It's not going to work.

We have to take the boat out into the deep waters to where the fish are. It is going to be uncomfortable and unsettling. There will be no easy answers. We will learn as much—if not more—about God and love and our faith, from those we are called to teach.

A guru was on his deathbed and his students were distraught. "Who will teach us now?" they asked him. He replied that he was just a finger pointing to the moon. They should look to the moon.

As the Church we are primarily the finger pointing to the reign of God in the kingdom. We should not allow people to mistake the Church for the kingdom. The Church just offers glimpses of it. Like effective parents, we have to guide, not dictate. We must point the way, accepting that sometimes the way is not clear and is open to question. Even though it can be incredibly frustrating to have to keep listening and discussing, when children know that their views are heard, respected, and understood, even if we do not agree with them, they are far more likely to listen, hear, and respect our views. It is surprising how, as they experience life, they come to appreciate, accept, and value what they learned from those who love them. Being a good parent is about being consistent and acknowledging what we don't know, rather than giving inadequate answers that are soon contradicted by our own behavior. It's about planting seeds and nurturing them, rather than demanding acceptance of your authority. Threats of exclusion simply mean that teenagers call your bluff and leave.

We need to have confidence that the Holy Spirit can do a much better job than we can at nurturing seeds, and we should ensure that the Spirit is invited into our lessons, discussions, and debates before we begin.

We should be welcoming questions even when we are uncertain of the answer, because revelation comes from what is not yet known. Everyone is called to accept co-responsibility for the apostolate, and unless we all accept that call instead of relying just on clergy to do the job, we will fail miserably in building up the Church. To achieve success we cannot rely only on our own gifts and talents. That is simply arrogance. Always, we should actively rely on the Holy Spirit to guide us, and we should ensure we are doing his will.

I am convinced that if the Church is to be relevant, thriving, and growing in the future, it will be because people will be questioning and the Church will be helping them to find the answers that are true. This will happen from cradle to grave, and the Church will be ever more relevant for it, because God stands up to scrutiny. Jesus promised us that so much more would be revealed to us, and a living, dynamic Church is open to that revelation:

> "I have much more to tell you, but you cannot bear it now. But when he comes, the Spirit of truth, he will guide you to all truth. He will not speak on his own, but he will speak what he hears, and will declare to you the things that are coming. He will glorify me, because he will take from what is mine and declare it to you. Everything that the Father has is mine; for this reason I told you that he will take from what is mine and declare it to you."
>
> JOHN 16:12-15

God stands up to scrutiny. We should never stop seeking to understand. We should never stop sharing what we have learned. It is just too important. Diarmaid MacCulloch ends his exhaustive *History of Christianity* with this: "Even those who see the Christian story as just that—a series of stories— may find sanity in the experience of wonder: the ability to listen and contemplate. It would be very surprising if this religion, so youthful, yet so varied in its historical experience, had now revealed all its secrets."

At the end of the last episode of the TV series of *A History of Christianity* on the BBC in 2009, MacCulloch concluded: "An old Dominican friend reminded me that Thomas Aquinas said that 'God is not the answer. God is the question.' As long as we keep asking the question, the Church cannot die."

For some, this chapter may be a bit depressing in that it identifies many reasons why we are not as effective as we would like to be in proclaiming the gospel. Instead, if we see it as identifying things that need to be challenged and perhaps indicate a positive way forward, it may give us hope, even if the work it identifies is not easy. I believe that change is an imperative. Working ever harder at doing more of the same will not produce a different result. We have to do things differently.

THREE

What is Church?
(And is it relevant?)

When I first started working in parish development, I assumed that everyone had the same understanding of what Church is—and of course I expected their understanding to be the same as mine. How wrong I was!

It seems obvious to me that if we are going to build up one, holy, catholic, and apostolic Church, the members of that Church ought to have a common understanding of what Church is. But I found that not only were there many differing viewpoints as to *what* Church is, there were also many different approaches to *how* we should be Church, and *why*.

Lots of research and lots of discussion did at last uncover an inclusive, holistic, balanced model of Church that is scripturally sound, and so far it seems to work.

So, what is Church?

Let's deal with the definition first. For me, Church is the way we, the People of God in the body of Christ, come together to live love to achieve Holy Communion with God and one another.

The Church is a way of life in which we pass the love of God to those around us so that they come to know God's love for them, and pass it along to others in turn. The way we live our faith defines Church for others: "'Rabbi...where do you live?' He replied, 'Come and see'; so they went and saw where he lived, and stayed with him that day. It was about the tenth hour....these two... became followers of Jesus...'" (John 1:38–40, NJB).

Like these two who went to see where and how Jesus lived, and by his example chose to follow him, the lives we live as followers of Christ should in turn lead others to him. Church reflects the life and mission of the People of God.

Coming forth from the eternal Father's love, founded in time by Christ the Redeemer and made one in the Holy Spirit, the Church has a saving and an eschatological purpose which can be fully attained only in the future world. But she is already present in this world, and is composed of [people], that is, of members of the earthly city who have a call to form the family of God's children during the present history of the human race, and to keep increasing it until the Lord returns. United on behalf of heavenly values and enriched by them, this family has been "constituted and structured as a society in this world" by Christ, and is equipped "by appropriate means for visible and social union." Thus the Church, at once "a visible association and a spiritual community," goes forward together with humanity and experiences the same earthly lot which the world does. She serves as a leaven and as a kind of soul for human society as it is to be renewed in Christ and transformed into God's family.

GAUDIUM ET SPES, #40

So together, we are all God's family—a creative, life-giving relationship—and the image and likeness of God. How would a
well-functioning family behave?

- It should have a common purpose—to love and care for
  one another and others in the society to which it belongs.
- All members should be unconditionally included in the
  loving relationship—a community of love.
- It should learn and teach knowledge, skills, and capabilities to further the common good of the family and the society to which it belongs.
- It should do the work of caring for one another within the
  community and in society.
- It should share what it has with each other and those who
  need it.

Can this same approach apply to the Church? *Models of the
Church*, the seminal work by Cardinal Avery Dulles (originally
written in 1974, revised and expanded in 1987 and 2002), identified six models of Church. In this work, he examined the different models, identified strengths and weaknesses of each, and
made recommendations. (See the Appendix for a summary of
the strengths and weaknesses—and proposed remedies—for his
models.) His models of Church are:

- The Church as Sacrament (Worship centered round the
  sacraments)
- The Church as Herald (Proclaiming)
- The Church as Servant (Service)
- The Church as Mystical Communion
- The Church as Institution
- The Church: A Community of Disciples

Dulles recommended a balance between those models that represented the life and mission of the Church—Sacrament, Herald, Servant, and Community—guided and supported by the Institutional Church.

This inclusive integration of models was clearly getting close to what I was looking for, but it was not quite fully there in terms of how to be Church. In his book *The Purpose-Driven Church* (Warren, 1995), Rick Warren looked to the Great Teachings for inspiration on what Church should be. This proved to be a good model to follow, because Jesus stressed these teachings himself.

When Jesus asked what the greatest commandment was, he said: "You shall love the Lord, your God, with all your heart, with all your soul, and with all your mind. This is the greatest and the first commandment. The second is like it: You shall love your neighbor as yourself" (Mt 22:37–39). He then emphasized the importance of this teaching by saying: "The whole law and the prophets depend on these two commandments" (Mt 22:40).

In other words, if we fail to love God, our neighbor, and our self, the rest is just words. Unfortunately, all too often it is in the nature of humankind to want to ritualize our communal relationship with God and our neighbor to a point where the meaning is lost. A good friend of mine remarked to me that "the Word was made flesh, and ever since we have been trying to turn him back into words."

After the Resurrection Christ gave us another great teaching that we should pay attention to because of the emphasis he placed on it. The instruction was The Great Commission: "Go, therefore, and make disciples of all nations, baptizing them in the name of the Father, and of the Son, and of the holy Spirit, teaching them to observe all that I have commanded you. And behold, I am with you always, until the end of the age" (Mt 28:19–20).

Of course all of Jesus' commands, that we need to teach, can all be summed up in this commandment to us: "This is my commandment: love one another, as I love you" (John 15:12).

And so, in the Great Commandment and the Great Commission we are told to

- Love God
- Love our neighbor as we love our self
- Make others aware of God's love for them
- Welcome them into the body of Christ
- And *teach* them to love God, love their neighbor as themselves, make others aware of God's love for them, and then welcome those people into the body of Christ.

I realized I had found the inclusive, holistic, balanced model of Church I was looking for. There are five clear pastoral purposes in this model that are interdependent, and together they are the life and mission of the Church. They provide a cohesive and comprehensive approach to Church that is totally focused on carrying out Christ's great teachings: The Great Commandment and The Great Commission.

WORSHIP the Lord *"You shall love the Lord, your God, with all your heart, with all your soul, and with all your mind"*

WELFARE of others *"You shall love your neighbor as [you love] yourself."*

Share the WORD *"Go and make disciples of all nations..."*

WELCOME all into Christ's Church *"Baptize them in the name of the Father, the Son and the Holy Spirit."*

Grow in WISDOM *"Teach them to observe all that I have commanded."*

Four of these purposes relate directly to Dulles' models of Church, viz.,

Sacrament	→	**WORSHIP**
Servant	→	**WELFARE**
Herald	→	**WORD**
Community	→	**WELCOME**

Dulles did not specifically identify a learning/teaching model, probably because that is still uncommon in many parts of the Catholic Church. While the Catholic Church has probably educated more people in its schools and universities than any other body on this planet to date, faith and ministry formation for anyone other than the clergy and religious effectively ends after confirmation (if not after First Communion), and becomes limited to the Sunday homily. This is not enough for Catholics to proclaim the gospel in a free, well-educated, questioning society.

But if we add lifelong learning and teaching—WISDOM—to Dulles' other four pastoral models of Church, and we exercise all five purposes in a holistic and balanced way, we will truly be the Community of Disciples he envisioned, because the purpose of a disciple of Christ is to worship, learn, and work to live and share a life in Christ, in community.

All five purposes are interdependent. If any purpose is weak or not practiced, it will undermine our effectiveness as Church.

At WORSHIP, in receiving the Holy Eucharist, we allow Christ to rise in us to go out as his hands and feet and voice to serve him in our neighbor, share the good news, and build up the body of Christ.

We do this by ensuring that all members are always WELCOME in a warm, inviting, accepting, and joyful community where we support each other on our pilgrimage to the kingdom. When new members are welcomed into communion at baptism, they receive the seeds of their gifts to build up the body of Christ.

We seek WISDOM to grow in confidence in our faith and to discern and nurture our gifts to maturity. Part of wisdom is recognizing our lack of knowledge, seeking that knowledge, and then using it for good. It is not about intellectual capability.

Because of our ever-improving confidence in faith and maturity of our gifts, we gain the courage and sustainable desire to go out and care for the WELFARE of others.

As a result of our example in caring for others and our confidence in faith, others are drawn to us and we are able to share the WORD with them, and in turn they may receive a call from the Holy Spirit.

Hearing that call, we WELCOME them into the Church in baptism. We worship with them in communion and encourage them to grow in wisdom to care for others, proclaim the good news, and welcome even more into communion in Christ's Church.

If any purpose is weak, it impacts on the rest and undermines our capability to build up the People of God in the body of Christ as the Temple of the Holy Spirit.

If people have no opportunity to grow in WISDOM, their faith will be poorly sustained, and they will have little confidence or desire to develop their gifts to serve others.

If people don't care for the WELFARE of others, there is no outward sign of God's love for us, and we fail to pass on that love. We fail to live our faith. We become a church of "do as I say, not as I do."

Without that example of living our love, few will be drawn to us, and we will fail to share the WORD, even with our children.

When we fail to do that, families, society, and the Church will all be weakened. If our WELCOME is poor, we will not be a community, and all our efforts at mission will be undermined. Not only will the newly baptized not stick around, but we will also encourage our existing members to leave.

If we fail to WORSHIP well, then we cut ourselves off from the source of all we need to live and to be love so that we can find peace, contentment, and joy in this life and the next.

There is nothing new here. From ancient times the Church has had five key practices:

Leiturgia *(Worship the Lord)*

Koinonia *(Welcome all into communion)*

Didache *(Teach / Grow in Wisdom)*

Diakonia *(Care for the Welfare of others)*

Kerygma *(Proclaim the Word)*

We have just not been good at recognizing their interdependence in building up an effective Church. When we recognize the interdependence between these purposes, it becomes obvious that they are in fact a formula for success in all aspects of life. In fact, these also sound much the same as the five behaviors of an effective family I identified earlier in the chapter.

I believe that this holistic and balanced approach to Church will also go a long way to meeting the challenge of Pope Benedict XVI's message to the Rome conference on the Laity, on May 26, 2009, mentioned earlier.

Over the next five chapters, we'll explore each of the five purposes in some detail.

FOUR

Worship (Leiturgia)

I n our communal worship Catholics actually receive the Body and Blood of Our Lord, Jesus Christ, in the Holy Eucharist. Why are our churches not packed? Is our worship so ritualized that we have lost its meaning? Have we so successfully locked God up in the tabernacle that we have turned the Flesh into words?

If we claim to be God's chosen people, then we have the responsibility of fulfilling God's purpose in choosing us. God's purpose for us is to serve others and share the good news that they too have been chosen for his work. The purpose of our worship is to renew and strengthen the bonds of our relationship with God and each other so that we are fortified and sustained for our mission together. Love can only remain love when it is passed on, because love is the action of God in us. If we refuse to act to pass it on, we reject the gift of that love.

■ The Mass and Mission

Occasionally, I have been fortunate enough to attend a Mass where the whole community is in Holy Communion with Christ and one another, and I see what our worship is intended to be.

I leave the Mass fired up with Christ in me. I am filled with joy and courage and desire to do his work. Sadly, we don't always celebrate the Mass in this way.

In too many parishes baptism is seen only as a rite of passage that enables access to the Holy Eucharist, and the Holy Eucharist is seen as an end in itself. After all, logic seems to question, what more could we possibly want or need than to receive the Body and Blood of our Lord Jesus Christ?

It is not possible to experience the Holy Eucharist as the summit of our faith unless we are one with God and each other—body, mind, and soul—in a Holy Communion of love. This does not happen simply by receiving the Holy Eucharist, but it can happen when we carry out Jesus' commandment to love one another as he loves us and then receive the Holy Eucharist together as a holy, loving community.

The Holy Eucharist is our greatest call to Christ's mission as spelled out by Jesus at the Last Supper.

When our children leave home to make their own way in life, as parents we realize how inexperienced they are, and we remind them of all we have taught them to prepare them for life. From John's gospel, it is clear that at the Last Supper Jesus felt the need to remind the disciples of everything he had taught them. If we accept that a Holy Communion with God can only be achieved through Jesus, then this summary of his teaching at the Last Supper clarifies the meaning of the Way, the Truth, and the Life:

> "Do you realize what I have done for you? You call me 'teacher' and 'master,' and rightly so, for indeed I am. If I, therefore, the master and teacher, have washed your feet, you ought to wash one another's feet. I have given

you a model to follow, so that as I have done for you, you
should also do." JOHN 13:12-15

Three times Jesus repeats his commandment "love one another
as I have loved you" (Jn 13:34; 15:12; 15:17). He tells us that it is by
our love for one another that we will be recognized as his disciples
(Jn 13:35), and he makes it clear that this is the fruitful work he
expects of us.

"It was not you who chose me, but I who chose you and
appointed you to go and bear fruit that will remain, so that
whatever you ask the Father in my name he may give you.
This I command you: love one another." JOHN 15:16-17

Jesus is passionate about us continuing his work because he
wants all of humanity to know the love of God. By loving one
another we come to be in a close personal relationship with him.

"Whoever has my commandments and observes them
is the one who loves me. And whoever loves me will be
loved by my Father, and I will love him and reveal myself
to him." JOHN 14:21

Jesus is under no illusions about how difficult it is for people to
live his message of love. He emphasizes the need for us to always
remain in him and with him:

"Remain in me, as I remain in you. Just as a branch cannot
bear fruit on its own unless it remains on the vine, so nei-
ther can you unless you remain in me. I am the vine, you are
the branches. Whoever remains in me and I in him will bear
much fruit, because without me you can do nothing."
JOHN 15:4-5

For most of us, words are rarely enough. We need more—something really tangible that lets us feel that Christ's unity with us is closer than our own heartbeat. Jesus knows that if we truly believe that we are one with him, then we are likely to choose to continue his work through him, with him, and in him. This is why he dramatically invites us to eat and drink his Body and Blood in the Holy Eucharist, to become his body, to carry on the work he started. Through his work we become love, so that we can become one with God.

Jesus' teaching at the Last Supper gives a very clear meaning and purpose to the Holy Eucharist. Jesus did not ask us to lock him up in a tabernacle and adore him. The Holy Eucharist enables us to become his body in a Holy Communion, to go out to love one another as he loves us, by healing the sick, clothing the naked, feeding the hungry, visiting prisoners, seeking justice for all, and caring for his creation.

The parish has a clear responsibility to enable, encourage, and support us all to allow Christ to rise again in us to carry out his commandment, so that we may learn to become love as God is love.

Every Mass is a call to mission: "Go and announce the Gospel of the Lord," or "Go in peace, glorifying the Lord by your life." These are not just words, but how many of us actually expect people to take these words to heart and act? We often have very low expectations of the members of our Church. Are we afraid to challenge them too much? Are we fearful that they will take their wallets and leave to join the parish down the road that is less demanding? The irony is that the collection plate fills up when people are encouraged and enabled to actively live their faith. We need to be driven by our hopes and dreams, not our fears.

■ Children

I am convinced that the degree to which we accept and welcome children and young people directly affects the participation and communion of our worship. Children can more easily open us to love. Jesus knew what he was talking about when he told us to become as little children.

A few years ago I was visiting my family in Australia, and my son mentioned that their parish priest had a reputation for building up parishes. I made a point of asking the priest what his secret was. His first response was surprise that he apparently had that reputation, but he thought for a minute or so and then said to me: "I insist on everyone making children welcome."

They had just built a lovely, big, bright new church, and every Mass I attended while on holiday was full, with an even attendance across all the generations. I attended the parish's annual general meeting, and I was very impressed with the quality of the office bearers, again with a good balance of membership across the generations.

In 2009 I attended the children's Mass at a church in Cambridge, UK. It is a big church and it was close to full. The children read the readings and gathered on the steps at the homily. Young children were altar servers. At the consecration the children all gathered around the altar. The singing was upbeat and joyful. As I left, there was a bounce to my step and a smile on my face. We all smiled and greeted complete strangers and congratulated the children. I felt good for the rest of the day.

■ Music

Young people also hunger for love. Make it easy for them to experience the love of Christ. Make the Mass more accessible. Smile and welcome them. Introduce yourself. Make sure there is someone of their own age to explain what is going on in the Mass. Sing hymns that are joyful and upbeat. Have drums and a beat to the music. Display the words of the hymn overhead on a screen. Make sure the homily is life-giving and relates the gospel to their lives.

Don't wait until the young people are already there before you change the style of the Mass. That way you will never have enough young people to justify the change. Behave as if they are already there, and they will hear about it. Involve the few young people that may be there. Get their advice and guidance. Don't do what you think they should like. Do what they actually do enjoy. It does not have to compromise our message. The gospel is relevant in any culture because every culture understands love.

The Sunday evening youth Mass at my former parish in Johannesburg, South Africa, had an attendance of close to 2,000, and fewer than half of the attendees were under thirty years of age. It was listed in the secular newspapers as one of the ten best things to do in Johannesburg on a weekend, whether you were Catholic or not. I loved the youth Mass because of the real sense of joy, spirituality, and communion—and the upbeat, joyful music.

Wherever I have experienced a growing, active community, music that appeals to all generations has always been a key part of worship. One parish priest I know considers it to be a failure if the congregation does not leave the Mass joyful, smiling, and ready to carry out the mission they are called to. He considers upbeat music and especially the final hymn to be critical in support of this. Mass attendance in his parish has grown by fifty percent in the last three years, and over thirty percent of the parishioners are engaged in active ministry.

We have to continue to engage with culture, as the Church has done since it was founded, and embrace those parts of culture that enable us to spread the good news without compromising our message. The Truth remains the Truth even if it is celebrated with rock music.

■ Prayer

Prayer is a key form of worship but many of us struggle to pray. We mouth the words of prayers learned in childhood, or we read words in books, often out of a sense of obligation or ritual. Even when we are hurting and need to be close to God, many repeat the same words over and over as if God can't understand or is somewhat deaf or perhaps asleep. Like little children we feel the louder we shout, the more attention we will get. We have not learned to stop "shouting" and to relax and enjoy the peace and comfort of just being aware of his presence with us, in our messy lives.

Joan Chittister, in *Called to Question*, has some challenging things to say about prayer:

> The purpose of prayer is simply to transform us to the mind of God. We do not go to prayer to coax God and the Cornucopia to make our lives a Disneyland of possibilities. We don't go to prayer to get points off our sins. We go to prayer to be transfigured ourselves, to come to see the world as God sees the world, to practice the presence of God, to put on a heart of justice, of love, and of compassion for others. We go to become a new soul.

The irony of prayer is that every act of prayer itself can delude us into thinking that we are spiritual people. If prayer is a recitation for the sake of ritual, then it is possible to pray and pray and never change at all. If prayer is not a spiritual vending machine, it is also not meant to be an escape from life. Every spiritual faddist wants it to be so, of course. But if prayer becomes the way we give ourselves permission to escape from the life around us, it is not prayer. It is some kind of self-induced hypnotism, at best. Real prayer plunges us into life, red and raw. It gives us new eyes. It shapes a new heart within us. It leaves us breathless in the presence of the living God. It makes demands on us—to feed the hungry and clothe the naked, give drink to the thirsty and take care of the sick. It requires that we become the hands of the God we say we have found.   PP. 46-47

Wow! Now that's what I call being aligned with God. It's an immediate demand to turn to your neighbor in service so that we can find the joy that Jesus promised us. WORSHIP is the key enabler for us to carry out the other four purposes so that we can live love.

■ Over-emphasizing WORSHIP

However, if your parish over-emphasizes some aspects of WORSHIP at the expense of the other pastoral purposes, it can undermine your ability to effectively build up the Church. If you recognize your parish as having most of the following symptoms, you need to build up the other pastoral purposes to become an effective community of disciples.

- Active membership is most likely to be interpreted within the parish as only meaning attendance at Mass.

- Only the faithful few, less than ten percent of the parishioners, are involved in ministry and prayer groups.

- Most of the ministries are inwardly focused and are centered around the church and Mass—readers, extraordinary ministers of Holy Communion, sacristan, altar servers, flower arrangers, cleaners, counters, administrators, or being involved in teas and fundraising, etc.

- Parish social activities are likely to have a fundraising element, and success is mostly determined by how much money is made.

- Other than for the faithful few, most parishioners are not involved in any other activities in the parish besides Sunday Mass and then not necessarily every Sunday.

- Most adult parishioners do not engage in any form of ongoing learning in their faith, outside of the Sunday homily.

- There is little if any conscious effort to evangelize within the parish.

- There are more funerals than baptisms in the parish.

- The sixteen-to-thirty-year-old age group is disproportionately absent from the parish even when this is not caused by demographic movement for tertiary study and migration to the cities.

- If people are not in a state of grace, there is not much else besides Mass being offered, and they tend to feel excluded from the Church.

- When relationships break down and people get divorced, they often feel excluded from the community.

- Fifty percent or more of parishioners are likely to be over fifty years of age, and this proportion is increasing.

- Membership is steadily declining.

FIVE

Welcome (Koinonia)

I recently went for coffee after Mass in another parish where everyone sat down at small tables chatting with their family or old friends. Despite my ability to speak comfortably in public, I am a natural introvert and I find it very difficult to strike up a conversation with a stranger or join a group unless I am invited to do so. I stood around alone for a while, feeling like a spare part, finished my coffee, and left.

Not long ago I heard of a funeral where a number of members of the deceased person's family were deaf. The priest refused to allow someone to sign for them from the sanctuary as apparently it was distracting to him and the congregation. They had to move to the side of the church. In another parish, the priest signs at every Mass, and there is a signing ministry for hearing people, to ensure everyone can fully participate. It is a joy to experience the communion across the entire community that is engendered as a result. Every effort is made to ensure inclusiveness for everyone.

After forty years of marriage, a good friend of mine divorced her husband. She had finally reached a stage where she could no longer continue with the stress and mental abuse she had endured for decades. As a result, she no longer felt welcome in her parish. In her time of need, she was deserted by her community. Her church had nothing to offer her by way of support and unconditional love. Surely this is a time when we should be most welcoming?

A man recently commented to me about how welcoming his parish was when people arrived at Mass. Knowing the age profile of his community, I asked him, perhaps unfairly, how welcome the youngsters who line up to enter the nearby nightclub would feel if they had to cross the road at the Easter Vigil and join the procession from the Service of Light into the Church. His response was that the youngsters would have to make some adjustments to their expectations and do something about their dress.

Is the "People who are different from us are not welcome" sign up over the church door? Or is it "Everyone is welcome provided they fit in with the way things are done and the way we behave around here"? Our welcome needs to be fully inclusive. People do not have to change in order to meet Christ. They change as a result of getting to know him and building a relationship with him.

One parish priest I know believes that welcome begins in the hall, not the church. He strives to make sure that the parish hall is a center for the entire community. At the parish festival, local people, Catholic or not, can rent space, put up a stand, and sell their own (appropriate) products. Even the police have a stand to share information and engage with the community. His point is that Catholics are so often misrepresented in the press and we are misunderstood by so many who know nothing of our faith, that secular people are often distrustful of us. By making the parish a center for the community, people can engage with and get to know us in the context of us living our faith.

This parish has also separated social activities from fundraising so nobody is financially excluded from any functions. Success is determined by the number attending and the way they enjoyed themselves, rather than the amount of money that was raised. Fundraising activities are clearly identified as such so there is no confusion.

■ Taking a look at our welcoming

Let's return for a moment to the example I mentioned above of the "welcoming" parish where youngsters would have to work to fit in. Why would youngsters want to join a bunch of strangers, mostly old folk, singing what to them seem like dirges from hundreds of years ago, standing up and kneeling down for no apparent reason, saying unfamiliar prayers together by heart, and sitting on hard benches in a dark and dreary building? Why would they want to do this if they are otherwise ignored except for a handshake halfway through, where the other person does not even look you in the eye and smile, let alone ask your name?

What is familiar? What is welcoming? What can they relate to? How can they participate when they don't know what is going on? Where's the joy in that? And why this focus on young people? Because they are or will soon be the parents of the next generation. If they aren't active and have no faith to pass on, it is just a matter of time before our churches will close. Something to consider: Is at least twenty-five percent of your parish council consistently under the age of thirty?

Will this change in focus chase away the older folk? Some may be upset but it has been my experience that young people and children are more likely to encourage parents who no longer practice their faith to return. Young people have idealism and an infectious energy that is very attractive and very effective at evangelization. Within reason, give them the freedom to do things their way, and find ways to say yes to their suggestions. Trust in the Holy Spirit. He just loves getting young people going, and they love his leadership.

Our welcome is affected by so many aspects of parish life, and I hope this chapter has already raised some questions about the things we often do without thinking that affect the welcome we offer to all of God's people.

Without an effective WELCOME, all our other efforts at building up the Church will be undermined quickly. However, if your parish over-emphasizes WELCOME at the expense of the other purposes, it can also undermine your ability to effectively build up the Church in your parish. If you recognize your parish as having most of the following symptoms, you need to look at building up the other pastoral purposes to become an effective community of disciples.

- Twenty to thirty percent or more of parishioners are actively involved in a strong social community in the parish, but little else.
- If anyone is not part of the "in" social group, they are largely isolated and alone.
- There are frequent socials of some sort at the drop of a hat but beyond that, little else.
- There is always a struggle to get volunteers for anything that is not related to the social life of the parish.
- There are no classes, retreats, or Bible study groups.
- Evangelization is something the Pentecostals and Baptists do.
- Membership is probably stagnant or declining.

SIX

Wisdom (Didache)

Growing in Wisdom is about three key things: continually growing in our relationship with Christ; discerning what our gifts are and how best to use them; and trying continually to improve our efforts to be of service to others.

■ Continually growing in our relationship with Christ

In some parts of the Church we still suffer from the legacy of a time when the laity were instructed only in those aspects of the faith that the institution considered necessary for them to know. Up until the 1940s, members of the laity were actively discouraged from reading the Bible for fear they would not be able to interpret it adequately. In my work I still come across many who are fearful of any learning that is not provided by a priest or a religious. Even a trained lay catechist is viewed with suspicion.

As a result, many members of the laity are just not able to pass on the faith in a challenging, questioning society. How many of us have been questioned about our faith by a colleague at work and have had the conversation interrupted by another Catholic who advances views that are incorrect and frankly embarrassing in their triumphalism? And is this the message we are passing along to our children?

We need to get past this barrier as quickly as possible, and accept our responsibility to seek the truth as guided by Vatican II:

> Man has been made by God to participate in this law, with the result that, under the gentle disposition of divine Providence, he can come to perceive ever more fully the truth that is unchanging. Wherefore every man has the duty, and therefore the right, to seek the truth in matters religious in order that he may with prudence form for himself right and true judgments of conscience, under use of all suitable means.
>
> Truth, however, is to be sought after in a manner proper to the dignity of the human person and his social nature. The inquiry is to be free, carried on with the aid of teaching or instruction, communication and dialogue, in the course of which men explain to one another the truth they have discovered, or think they have discovered, in order thus to assist one another in the quest for truth.
>
> Moreover, as the truth is discovered, it is by a personal assent that men are to adhere to it. On his part, man perceives and acknowledges the imperatives of the divine law through the mediation of conscience. In all his activity a man is bound to follow his conscience in order that he may come to God, the end and purpose of life. It follows that he is not to be forced to act in manner contrary to his conscience. Nor, on the other hand, is he to be restrained from acting in accordance with his conscience, especially in matters religious. The reason is that the exercise of religion, of its very nature, consists before all else in those internal, voluntary and free acts whereby man sets the

course of his life directly toward God. No merely human power can either command or prohibit acts of this kind.

DIGNITATIS HUMANAE, #3

When we talk about ongoing lifelong learning, a common objection is that the parish does not have the money to pay for expensive programs and study courses. I encourage good programs and formal education where it is appropriate and affordable, but in truth we need nothing more than a Bible and a willingness to share our faith to engage in a process of growing in Christ together. Catechesis is an ancient and very effective way of sharing our faith.

We don't know when or how the Holy Spirit may touch people, but there are a few common signs that an encounter has occurred. People who have had an encounter want to understand more, and they want to put their newfound faith into action by developing a closer relationship with God, serving his people and sharing their experience with others. This is true for new members of the Church and also for those baptized as babies who later have a personal encounter with the Holy Spirit.

What happens if we stop there, and fail to continue our explorations deeper into the faith? Simple: this newfound faith can easily wither and die in the midst of all the pressures and distractions of the world around us. There is no point at which we graduate and know it all. If we stop questioning and learning and putting our knowledge into practice, our faith weakens. Research among evangelical churches has revealed that where churches are active only in the area of worship services, a mere sixteen percent of their members remain five years after joining. Where the Church is active in "Sunday School" or ongoing adult formation, eighty-three percent of members remain after five years (*Surprising Insight from the Unchurched and Proven Ways to Reach Them*, Thom Rainer, 2001).

Without ongoing catechesis, the vast majority of us will not venture into caring for others as a way of practicing our faith and proclaiming the gospel. And such catechesis must relate what we learn to the experience of our own life. The *National Directory for Catechesis* states: "Catechesis links human experience to the revealed word of God, helping people to ascribe Christian meaning to their own existence. It enables people to explore, interpret, and judge their basic experience in the light of the gospel. Catechesis helps them relate the Christian message to the most profound questions in life: the existence of God, the destiny of the human person, the origin and end of history, the truth about good and evil, the meaning of suffering and death, and so forth" (p. 98).

In addition, it is crucial that we make a point of taking time to stop and reflect on our pilgrimage to the kingdom. Martineau, Weber, and Kehrwald make the point in *Intergenerational Faith Formation* that "one of the abilities needed to link the human experience to the Christian message is the ability to reflect—the ability to stop, look, and listen to the moment just experienced or about to be experienced. Reflection is almost a lost art in our Christian communities and is an art that needs learning and practicing across the generations if we are to remain connected to our identity as disciples" (Mariette Martineau et al., 2008, p. 46).

If we fail to relate our ongoing learning to our lives or we fail to stop and reflect to discern meaning, the practice of our faith and prayer life can easily descend into meaningless ritual.

We grow in knowledge and confidence by sharing our own experience of Christ with others and in turn relating their experience to our own lives. Through others we come to recognize the validity of our own experience and understand the value that it has in proclaiming the gospel. This *echoing* of our experience of faith is catechesis. Benedict XVI makes this clear:

> How can we make knowledge of God accessible to people? God's speaking to us reaches us through men and women who have listened to God and come into contact with God; ...for whom God has become an actual experience and who as it were know him at first hand. So the element of trust works here too; faith forms a network of mutual dependence, solidarity, where we rely on others who have direct experience of God. 'He who has seen me has seen the Father' (Jn 14:9) applies to us all.
>
> *THE YES OF JESUS CHRIST,* 2005

Sadly, there are still too many people who believe that catechesis means studying nothing more than the *Catechism of the Catholic Church.*

Practicing the pastoral purpose of growing in WISDOM, continual learning, and using that knowledge for good, is the key to opening the door to a holistic, inclusive, balanced, more effective model of church that is committed to evangelization. When we understand and accept why we should do things, rather than just being told they are good for us, we choose willingly to do those things. As a result, we are more committed, and our improved understanding makes us more effective as a Church that sets an example that people want to follow. Our task, in deepening our understanding of God, is to keep learning and experiencing God so we can remain motivated to become unconditional love as God is, and thereby become one with him.

The Church clearly recognizes that the effectiveness of catechesis is not just in teaching the recently converted but also in developing the maturity and sustaining the faith of the entire community.

> The Christian community not only gives much to those who are being catechized but also receives much from them. New converts, especially adolescents and adults, in adhering to Jesus Christ, bring to the community which receives them new religious and human wealth. Thus the community grows and develops. Catechesis not only brings to maturity the faith of those being catechized but also brings the community itself to maturity.
>
> *GENERAL DIRECTORY FOR CATECHESIS*
> © LIBRERIA EDITRICE VATICANA, 1997, P. 146

There is no reason for fear in encouraging everyone to question and explore their faith in much greater depth. It is something to be done from cradle to grave and, ideally, intergenerationally, in the parish, and at home. Each parish should have a small ministry group that has the ministry of Family Mission to assist families in this effort and more.

Couldn't this kind of exploration lead to misperceptions and misunderstandings about the faith? No. It is not difficult to determine if you're going in the right direction. If your explorations lead to fear or a sense of being manipulated or a need for power over others—even if you consider that to be for their own good—then it is not from God. If you feel led to a desire to serve without expecting anything in return, to kindness, caring, virtue, tolerance, and open-mindedness, then you are on the path to unconditional love, which is a clear sign of the presence of God.

I have found that no matter how rigorous my questioning, as long as I keep an open mind, God stands up to scrutiny. Our questioning leads to greater understanding, which leads to greater commitment, which makes us more effective in carrying out all five purposes of the Great Teachings; and so we build up Christ's

Church as he intended. This is not something we can do in isolation. We need to echo what we have learned and experienced to each other through catechesis so we all grow in understanding, maturity, and commitment. As we grow in our understanding of Christ, we will naturally seek to live a better life in Christ. To do this, we need to understand our purpose in the body of Christ. We come to understand our purpose or our role in the body of Christ by discerning and understanding how to use the gifts we are given.

▓ Discerning our gifts

At Easter we rejoice when people are baptized into the Church, but when we look around for these same people at Mass a few months later, we don't see them. What's going on?

We mentioned before the danger involved when we regard the Holy Eucharist purely as the summit of our faith and ignore the fact that it is also its source. When this happens, we offer little else beyond the Holy Eucharist to new members. They sense that they have received gifts at baptism, but there is little opportunity for them to discern what those gifts are, and there are fewer opportunities to put them into practice to build up the Church. They felt a call to join the Church, they received gifts, and they were left hanging. Where anybody is doing anything, it is often a closed clique and new members are not welcome.

How do we discern what gifts we have received? How do we develop those gifts? How do we know what our purpose is in the Church, the body of Christ?

> For as in one body we have many parts, and all the parts do not have the same function, so we, though many, are one body in Christ and individually parts of one another.

> Since we have gifts that differ according to the grace
> given to us, let us exercise them: if prophecy, in pro-
> portion to the faith; if ministry, in ministering; if one is a
> teacher, in teaching; if one exhorts, in exhortation; if one
> contributes, in generosity; if one is over others, with dili-
> gence; if one does acts of mercy, with cheerfulness...Do
> not grow slack in zeal, be fervent in spirit, serve the Lord.
>
> ROMANS 12:4-8, 11

Instead of simply throwing people off a cliff at baptism and
(perhaps) expecting them to fly, they should be supported to discern what their gifts are and encouraged and assisted to put their
gifts into practice by joining a ministry within the parish.

There are a number of tools and techniques that positively aid
the process of discerning gifts. This may be difficult to do in a
small parish, but one of the beauties of being the Catholic Church
is that we can collaborate with other parishes or set up this capability at a deanery or diocesan level if the resources of a parish are
limited.

■ Continually improving the quality of ministry

Having discerned our gifts, it is not enough to simply work hard
in our ministry. If we keep our head down and keep working
without reflection on what we are trying to achieve and how we
are going about it, we can waste a lot of effort without achieving
any significant benefit.

To grow in wisdom, you will have some of your most treasured
values challenged.

Some years ago good friends of mine adopted a young AIDS
orphan who was being cared for in an orphanage run by members of a religious order. As part of their ethos, these sisters

remain as poor as the people they help, and work as hard as they do. No doubt this helps in understanding and relating to the pain of the poor.

There were six young babies of a similar age in the group from which the boy was adopted, and they were all left in a single cot, apparently without any physical contact from caregivers outside of feeding times. Over the next two years, four of these babies died, and only one little boy in the home remained alive. My friends could bear it no longer and adopted him as well.

Although he was over two years of age, when the second little boy arrived home, he could not yet walk, had not seen a toy, and had no idea how to get down three stairs into their lounge. He did not smile or laugh. Three months later he was transformed into a laughing, boisterous, affectionate little fellow, running around the house and garden, getting into everything, and creating chaos as only healthy, much loved little children can do.

My friends are convinced that the four little babies who didn't survive died from a lack of physical contact and love.

Both these little boys were starved for physical contact and affection while in the orphanage, because the sisters and their staff were so busy working hard at things like doing the laundry by hand. My friends offered to raise funds for washing machines, but this offer was refused because the poor around them could not afford appliances and they would undermine their ethos of solidarity with the poor.

Surely if these sisters, who are working themselves to the bone, just stopped to think and reflect on the effectiveness of their work, they would have to question the morality of babies dying for a lack of love because their hard and inefficient work, in order to maintain solidarity with the poor, allows them no time to hug and cuddle the babies.

The original idea may have been noble, indeed saintly, but the law of unintended consequences does not care how noble your purpose may be. All the consequences of our actions, both effective and ineffective, need to be considered. We cannot blindly follow rules without considering their overall impact.

No matter what our ministry, we should always be evaluating the effectiveness of our efforts and not be blind to both the benefits, which we should seek to maximize, and the unintended negative consequences, which we should seek to eliminate. If these unintended consequences are so grave that even our purpose in that ministry needs to be challenged, we should do so.

Growing in wisdom is challenging. We have to be clear on what our purpose is and be prepared to do whatever it takes to achieve that purpose. Before anyone misunderstands that statement, stop and ask whether striving to pass on the love of God and make him known to all of humankind (which is our key purpose) could be achieved effectively by doing anything that harmed or excluded those around us.

In discerning the quality of our service, we need to continually ask three questions:

- How effective is this in sharing the love of God?
- Does this in any way hinder us or anyone else from sharing the love of God?
- Is there a better way to more effectively share the love of God?

In this way we will grow in wisdom and gain the confidence necessary to go out to serve the Lord and proclaim the good news. Without confidence in our experience of Christ, our understanding of our faith, and our gifts, we will be reluctant to engage in ministry and mission to build up the body of Christ.

The pastoral purpose of growing in WISDOM is the key to engaging the Church in all five purposes. However, while growing in Wisdom is a key purpose of sustaining faith, if it is overemphasized at the expense of the other four purposes, there is a real risk of intellectual elitism leading to the exclusion of those with gifts in other areas of ministry. If this happens, it will undermine efforts to build community, serve others, proclaim the gospel, and worship in communion.

SEVEN

Welfare (Diakonia)

As the Father loves me, so I also love you. Remain in my love. If you keep my commandments, you will remain in my love, just as I have kept my Father's commandments and remain in his love. I have told you this so that my joy may be in you and your joy may be complete. This is my commandment: love one another as I love you. No one has greater love than this, to lay down one's life for one's friends. You are my friends if you do what I command you.

JOHN 15:9-14

Jesus demonstrated the greatest love anyone can have by dying on the cross for us. He set an example that he expects us to live up to when he tells us to love one another as he loves us. By his standards, he expects us to lay down our lives for our friends.

Hey! Steady now! That's a bit over the top! Is he really asking us to lay down our lives for others?

I can see him looking at me straight in the eye as he answers the question: "Yep. That sounds about right."

Laying down your life for others does not mean that you have to die for them, although that possibility is not excluded. Realistically, however, every minute of your life that is given to serve others is a minute you have laid down in love. It is a minute of your life that can never be replaced. It is gone forever. You have given yourself, the most generous gift we can give to another. This is the meaning of the greatest love: to give the best you have to offer, yourself. This is the perfect gift of himself that God gives to us—Love.

This is what it's all about. This is what it means to live love, so we can become love as God is love, in order to become one with him. This is the kingdom on earth, here and now, today, right here in our ordinary, messy, mundane lives. This is the secret to life, love, and the whole of creation. This is what it is to live the greatest love and become a living sacrament by passing on the love of God to others.

It is for this that Christ humbles himself in the Holy Eucharist to remind us in a tangible way of the gift of his love and friendship that he expects us to pass on and share through service to others.

What we speak of the Church as being the body of Christ, by implication we all have a different role to perform. If everyone wants to do the same thing, or if we fail to ensure that all functions of the Body are carried out, we will fail to be an effective church. A key role for pastors and teachers is to

> ...equip the holy ones for the work of ministry, for building up the body of Christ, until we all attain to the unity of faith and knowledge of the Son of God, to mature manhood, to the extent of the full stature of Christ, so that we may no longer be infants, tossed by waves and swept along by every wind of teaching arising from human trickery, from their cunning in the interests of deceitful scheming. Rather, living the truth in love, we should grow in every

way into him who is the head, Christ, from whom the
whole body, joined and held together by every supporting
ligament, with the proper functioning of each part, brings
about the body's growth and builds itself up in love.

EPHESIANS 4:12-16

It is not enough to exhort people at the end of Mass to "Go and
announce the Gospel of the Lord," or "Go in peace, glorifying the
Lord by your life." Where do they start? Without a plan of action
and guidance, few take this exhortation seriously, and nothing
gets done. What if everyone decided to do the same thing? Chaos
would ensue. If everyone does whatever they like on the building site of the Church, not much of a church will result. If everyone sits on the sidelines wondering what to do, nothing much is
going to be built. If we accept cash in place of effort, the money
will soon be misused on building physical churches and material
assets, rather than building up the body of Christ.

We don't equip anyone without a plan, unless we don't care
what it is they are to do. The desired end result should be clear,
and everyone involved should know what they have to do and
how that meshes with what the rest are doing.

It bears repeating: our job is to build up the body of Christ so
everyone can become fully mature with the fullness of Christ himself. The Church is not for God. God does not need the Church.
He is almighty and all-powerful and does not need anything or
anyone. All God wants to do is to love us and to encourage and
support every one of us to become the love that he is. The way we
do this is by building up the Church for each other—together. We
are all of us the Church, the people of God in the body of Christ.
It is God's generous gift to us to guide and help us in our quest to
become love.

The way we build up the Church is through ministry. We minister to each other and to all of God's creation. Many people still misunderstand what the word ministry means and assume it only relates to liturgy or to those officially ordained. To minister to others is to care for their welfare. Ministry is the passing on of God's love to others by laying down a part of our lives in service to them. We are called to ministry in every aspect of our lives as examples of the humanity that God created us to be:

> ...the laity, by their very vocation, seek the kingdom of God by engaging in temporal affairs and by ordering them according to the plan of God. They live in the world, that is, in each and in all of the secular professions and occupations. They live in the ordinary circumstances of family and social life, from which the very web of their existence is woven. They are called there by God that by exercising their proper function and led by the spirit of the Gospel they may work for the sanctification of the world from within as a leaven. In this way they may make Christ known to others, especially by the testimony of a life resplendent in faith, hope and charity. Therefore, since they are tightly bound up in all types of temporal affairs it is their special task to order and to throw light upon these affairs in such a way that they may come into being and then continually increase according to Christ to the praise of the Creator and the Redeemer.
>
> *LUMEN GENTIUM*, #31

We can care for the welfare of others by carrying out ministry in each of the five pastoral purposes as shown in the examples given in Chapter Eleven.

We should always remember that we do not serve others in order to convert them. We serve others just to share the love of God in the name of Christ our savior. We do not expect people to convert as a result, although we do hope for conversion in their lives, that they will become open to receiving the gift of faith. There are no conditions attached to God's love. People may ask why we do this (giving us an opportunity to share the good news), but that is not the purpose of our service. It is a free, unconditional gift of our own time. We should never use it to manipulate others by making them feel obligated.

With the potential for service available to us as disciples of Christ, it is clear that there is a place for everyone to use whatever their God-given gifts and talents are, to build up the Church. As everyone comes to use their gifts as intended, the Church "brings about the body's growth and builds itself up in love."

If as a Church we are fulfilling as many of these functions as we are able, not only within our parishes but in collaboration with the parishes and other churches around us to maximize our efforts, I don't think there will be any debate about the relevance of the Church in a twenty-first-century, affluent Western society.

If, however, your model of Church over-emphasizes WELFARE largely to the exclusion of the other purposes, there is a real danger that your parish will simply function as another welfare organization. It is not enough to do good deeds for our own self-gratification. We serve others in the name of Christ to bring about the kingdom and the reign of God. The Church is about living our relationship with God through Christ incarnate in our neighbor. It is about Holy Communion in Love.

EIGHT

Word (Kerygma)

Proclaiming the good news is another gift we have to share. It is an invitation to follow Christ as his disciple. Faith is not something that can be imposed or even freely given. It is a gift from God. We cannot *convert* anyone. But we can aid that conversion by inviting people to join us as a community learning how to live as Christ calls us to live: to be fully human.

In a narrow sense the outcome of evangelization is people coming to faith. But if that's as far as we go, then we ignore the fact that faith should bring about a transformation or conversion in the way we live. Conversion is a lifelong process and needs help. At a practical level, effective evangelization is about a partnership between the evangelizers and the Holy Spirit. Faith is a gift of the Holy Spirit. Without it people are unlikely to want to live a life in Christ. As evangelizers we don't have the power to give anyone the gift of faith, but we do have a responsibility to nurture and sustain the conversion process by inviting and supporting people to embark on the journey to become love, through discipleship in Christ, so all can be one in Holy Communion with God in his kingdom. We do this by sharing the gospel and supporting people in their quest to live their life in Christ. This is the way, the truth, and the life. Through discipleship we learn and support each other on our faith journey as a community. We become an effective Church through active discipleship.

Evangelization and catechesis are two sides of the same coin. At a practical level, they are both about inviting people into discipleship. Evangelization brings people to faith. Catechesis affirms and supports the sharing of our faith. Discipleship is about putting our faith into action. Love cannot be passive. We cannot claim to love a starving or naked person without doing something to help them. Effective evangelization and catechesis, in partnership with the Holy Spirit, should result in two outcomes; faith, which is a gift from the Holy Spirit, and activists for Christ—more disciples working hard to fulfil the mission of the Church to bring about the reign of God.

If our efforts at evangelization and catechesis create an expectation of living a life in Christ as his disciple rather than simply ending with baptism, that discipleship will enable people to mature in faith and give expression to it as Christ intended.

Conversion is a journey, not an event. To darken the doors of a church is, for many, a leap way too far from where they are at today. A clear example to illustrate this is the article in the *Telegraph* on December 18, 2010, about the impact that writing *The Nativity*, produced by the BBC in 2010, had on Tony Jordan, its author:

> "The only thing I know for sure is that the words I read as coming from Jesus Christ are the most truthful thing I have ever heard. As a blueprint for mankind, it is so smart that it couldn't even have come from a clever philosopher. Who would have been smart enough to say 'He who is without sin cast the first stone'? Wow! That's pretty cool." [The journalist notes that] writing *The*

Nativity may have converted him to the virgin birth, even to Jesus's blueprint, but it won't inspire Jordan to take his seat in the ancient church a few doors down from his house on December 25. "I have a distaste for people who say to me if you come through these doors, walk down this aisle, sit on that wooden bench, and sing these hymns in this order, I have got God in a little bottle under my pulpit and I'll let you have a look," he says. "I don't think [that] was God's intention." JORDAN, 2010

Religions are notorious for trying to put God in a bottle or a tabernacle. At one level it makes God safe and controllable. At another level it tempts those who have the keys to the tabernacle to try to become the intermediaries between God and the rest of us. In the not-too-distant past, it was not uncommon for many to believe that those who had the keys to the tabernacle had a clear duty to control who had access to God! (Occasionally, I still come across people who believe this.)

Things are changing but the pace of change from the old paradigm needs to accelerate in order for us to become more relevant in the world today.

The goal of evangelization is active discipleship: people following Christ, engaged in learning, and putting that learning into action in pastoral ministry. Evangelization invites people to start the courting stage of the relationship, without making deep commitments. It's about getting to know each other, working together, understanding values, and adjusting those values to the demands of a life in Christ.

People can be active disciples without being in communion with the Church because discipleship is about being in relationship, learning, and doing. Because our learning never ends, and it is in doing that we become love, we need to remain active disciples after baptism as well.

Many people are in communion but are not active disciples. A passive faith is like a branch on the vine that bears no fruit. We need help to remain active. The Holy Eucharist is our greatest call to mission, our greatest aid to mission, and our greatest celebration of mission. Even so, many fail to act on that call. James was quite vociferous in his assessment of an inactive faith: "Indeed someone may say, 'You have faith and I have works.' Demonstrate your faith to me without works, and I will demonstrate my faith to you from my works. You believe that God is one. You do well. Even the demons believe that and tremble. Do you want proof, you ignoramus, that faith without works is useless?...For just as a body without a spirit is dead, so also faith without works is dead" (Jas 2:18–20, 26).

Love is never passive. It is the action of God in us, and in faith we are called to release that action and pass on his love by serving others. The outward sign of any sacrament is our passing on the love of God to others. If we fail to act, the grace of God, that generous gift of his love, fails to be the sacrament he intended it to be.

So, clearly a community of disciples does not require that all members will be in communion in the Church, but every member should be an active disciple of Christ: building a community that is continually praying and worshiping, learning, serving, and sharing the good news. Carrying out the wishes of a totally generous God, the Church continually creates opportunities for all its members to come into communion.

This inclusive approach is practical because it recognizes that people do not blindly accept truth at face value. Faith needs to be supported by reason. Actions speak louder than words. Active discipleship provides the opportunity for people to experience the reality of a life in Christ before becoming receptive to the gift of faith from the Holy Spirit. By inviting people to belong before they believe, we are not doing anything new; it is exactly the approach Jesus used, when he invited people to follow him to discover what he was about.

Faith is born of the soul, not the body. Whoever would lead someone to faith needs the ability to speak well and to reason properly, without...threats.... BENEDICT XVI, *FAITH, REASON AND THE UNIVERSITY*

■ Evangelization and the stages of faith

It may be appropriate to consider this inclusive approach to membership in the context of the stages of faith that are summarized in the Appendix. I suggested that most of the free, educated members of our secular society, who expect to be able to think for themselves, are arguably in Stage 5. They have questioned and found the answers inadequate. Realistically, it is unlikely that we will persuade them to forget their questions and blindly accept a Stage 4 exclusive religion that only welcomes those who think as we do and does not encourage any questioning.

The way forward is Stage 6, where we recognize and accept that we are all on a pilgrimage to the kingdom. It is a journey into unknown territory. Nobody has all the answers to deal with the uncertainties and contradictions. Inevitably people will be at different places on the journey, and all of us from time to time will take a wrong turn. It is only through ongoing learning, keeping our focus firmly on Christ, and relying on the help and support of each other that we can successfully make this pilgrimage.

In Stage 6 questions are welcomed and answers are explored together. This is not to suggest that anyone is free to apply their own truth. There is but one Way, one Truth, and one Life—Jesus Christ in the context of a community of believers, his Church. We rely on the centuries of wisdom in the Church that reflect our ongoing relationship with God and each other, to guide us in our search for the Way, the Truth, and the Life. In that context our questions help us to understand what a relationship with God and each other means in the reality of our lives in the twenty-first century, which is a different society to the one that Jesus lived in 2,000 years ago.

■ Becoming a Community of Disciples

Those actively engaged in all five purposes will become a Community of Disciples. In reality, not everyone in a parish will be an active disciple. Many will simply remain in communion without being active disciples. We should not resent that; nor should they be made to feel that they are less worthy. While always ensuring that the door remains wide open for anyone to become a disciple, we should not judge those who do not accept the invitation. The pilgrimage to the kingdom is a journey; it is not possible for everyone in a parish to be in the same place on that journey. We should respect, accept, and meet people where they are on that journey.

With concerted effort, within five or six years it is possible to get thirty to forty percent of the parishioners actively involved across all five pastoral purposes. At this level of participation, you will be experiencing steady if not rapid growth in membership and active participation.

NINE

A community of disciples

What does it mean to say that one is a disciple, a follower of Christ? It's important to clarify this term, especially as is pertains to being a disciple in the context of a parish that is a Community of Disciples.

Originally in Judaism, a disciple was a student of a rabbi. Typically the disciple would choose which rabbi to follow based on their assessment of his understanding of the Law—the Torah. The student was there to learn so that one day he too could become a rabbi.

■ Disciples are chosen

Jesus' disciples did not choose him. He chose them: "It was not you who chose me, but I who chose you and appointed you to go and bear fruit that will remain..." (Jn 15:16).

Some wanted to join him but they did not meet his requirements for unconditional commitment and he did not accept them:

> As they were proceeding on their journey someone said
> to him, "I will follow you wherever you go." Jesus an-

swered him, "Foxes have dens and birds of the sky have
nests, but the Son of Man has nowhere to rest his head."
     And to another he said, "Follow me." But he replied,
"[Lord,] let me go first and bury my father." But he an-
swered him, "Let the dead bury their dead. But you, go
and proclaim the kingdom of God."
     And another said, "I will follow you, Lord, but first let
me say farewell to my family at home." [To him] Jesus
said, "No one who sets a hand to the plow and looks to
what was left behind is fit for the kingdom of God."

LUKE 9:57-62

Jesus' disciples did not necessarily fully believe before they belonged. They had accepted Jesus' call recognizing something that
needed to be explored—the way, the truth, and the life. Some followed him, tried it, and left. His apostles did not fully believe even
after three years of constant discipleship and close companionship with him. When the chips were down, most of them abandoned him at the crucifixion and doubted that he truly was the
Messiah. Jesus invited people to belong, learn, and act, without
requiring them to believe, although faith was and is clearly the
ultimate aim.

Today, the disciples of Jesus are a community of seekers, cat-
echumens, and those in full communion, praying, continually
learning, and being encouraged to put that learning into practice in pastoral ministry as examples of the Word in action. They
have been called by the Holy Spirit and have accepted that call
to start a lifelong journey of worship, learning, service, and sharing—together in community. The Holy Spirit is active in us with
a gift of faith long before we recognize and confess that we believe in Christ.

We can invite people to listen for the call of God and answer it. We can ask people to come and see and show them what a life in Christ is all about. We cannot appoint disciples. But as Church we can recognize those who have accepted that call and help each other to be effective disciples.

■ Disciples are both students and teachers

Jesus' disciples were also students, but not necessarily students of the Torah, the Law. They were students learning how to become love so that they could become one with God. In living that love by giving witness to Christ as they passed love on to others, they also became teachers. While Jesus made it clear that he did not come to throw out the Torah, he taught that love for our neighbor always took priority over the Law:

> Moving on from there, he went into their synagogue. And behold, there was a man there who had a withered hand. They questioned him, "Is it lawful to cure on the sabbath?" so that they might accuse him. He said to them, "Which one of you who has a sheep that falls into a pit on the sabbath will not take hold of it and lift it out? How much more valuable a person is than a sheep. So it is lawful to do good on the sabbath." Then he said to the man, "Stretch out your hand." He stretched it out, and it was restored as sound as the other. But the Pharisees went out and took counsel against him to put him to death.
>
> MATTHEW 12:9-14

Jesus was not attempting to turn his disciples into theologians. He was teaching them to do all he had done. He expected them all to give witness to him—the Way, the Truth, and the Life. Lifelong learning and teaching through witness to Christ—sharing our experience of him—are key characteristics by which we recognize disciples of Christ.

■ Disciples are activists doing Jesus' work

Following Jesus means that there is no work that disciples are unworthy to perform. They are not intended to be disciples for their own sake. They are called to do the work of the kingdom of God: feed the hungry, clothe the naked, heal the sick, teach, preach, evangelize, and proclaim the good news.

People are often uncomfortable when I talk about becoming an activist for Christ. They tend to assume that activism means accosting people at bus stops and trying to convert them on the spot. Anyone who does anything to reach out beyond themselves to others or to share the good news is an activist for Christ. As an example, the housebound person who prays for the work of the Church is an activist.

Christians are not immune to individualism and consumerism. When we as a Church promote the idea of saving our own souls as the reason for belonging to the Church, we promote a very self-centered, individualistic faith that is fueled by the norms of the society we live in. As a result, it is easy to be a black hole absorbing all the love that God showers on us, as we fail to pass that love on to others. In charity we speak of these people as having a private faith. In reality, love of God cannot be private. You can't do love alone. God's love has to be passed on. You can't love God if you don't love your neighbor, because God is in your neighbor.

If we are serious about being activists, no matter how humble our efforts, we can expect that the Holy Spirit will magnify those efforts and also stretch us to become more active. As our efforts bear fruit, we will naturally grow in confidence and want to become more active. The first step to activism is the prayer: *Here I am, Lord. Use me as you will.*

■ Disciples are missionaries

At the end of Chapter One, I stated that our mission as Church, indeed the meaning of our life, is to become love as God is love, so that we can all become one with him—a Holy Communion. In other words, our mission is to work to bring about God's kingdom of love—a new order through Christ, Our Lord:

> Consequently, from now on we regard no one according to the flesh; even if we once knew Christ according to the flesh, yet now we know him so no longer. So whoever is in Christ is a new creation: the old things have passed away; behold, new things have come. And all this is from God, who has reconciled us to himself through Christ and given us the ministry of reconciliation, namely, God was reconciling the world to himself in Christ, not counting their trespasses against them and entrusting to us the message of reconciliation.   2 CORINTHIANS 5:16-19

Disciples are recognized by how they engage in their mission to promote and sustain reconciliation with God and one another.

■ Disciples evangelize and catechize

Evangelization and catechesis are key to mission. They are the major activities in bringing about active discipleship through which we grow in faith and share the good news. We know that our mission can only be achieved through Jesus Christ. He is the Way, the Truth, and the Life. If we want to work to fulfill our mission we must do what Jesus taught us:

When Jesus, who had suffered the death of the cross for mankind, had risen, He appeared as the one constituted as Lord, Christ and eternal Priest, and He poured out on His disciples the Spirit promised by the Father. From this source the Church, equipped with the gifts of its Founder and faithfully guarding His precepts of charity, humility and self-sacrifice, receives the mission to proclaim and to spread among all peoples the Kingdom of Christ and of God and to be, on earth, the initial budding forth of that kingdom. While it slowly grows, the Church strains toward the completed Kingdom and, with all its strength, hopes and desires to be united in glory with its King.

LUMEN GENTIUM, #5

There are different forms of evangelization and catechesis, and not everyone has the same gifts to become active in the same way. Pat Collins, in his book *The Gifts of the Spirit* (2009), cites four approaches given by John Wimber (1934-1997) that for me clarify the ways in which we can use our gifts effectively to evangelize and sustain our faith.

The first approach is through *presence*. Being present to others in ordinary ways is a wonderful witness of our faith. Welcoming someone to a gathering with a lovely hot cup of coffee and a warm smile on a cold night is a great way of being active. Making sure the Church is clean and inviting for Mass is another. Another example of presence is to look someone in the eye at the sign of peace in Mass, smile, wish them peace, and be sure to introduce yourself after Mass if you don't know them.

The second approach is through *proclaiming*. Some people have the gift of being able to explain the gospel to others in the context of the world we live in today and make it really meaningful. Not everyone has this gift but we can all give credibility to this work when the people who have just heard the Word in this way see us living it by being present to them.

The third approach is through *persuasion*. The most effective form of persuasion to get others to want to live a life in Christ is by sharing our experience of Christ and what he has meant to us. When we experience Christ we witness his real presence and the effect he has on our lives. By being a witness in sharing that experience and allowing others to see how our lives have changed for the better as a result, we can be very persuasive.

The fourth approach is through *power*—the power of the Holy Spirit, that is. Sometimes the Holy Spirit gives us special gifts or charisms to use to build up the Church. The days of miracles are not over. Reports of miraculous healing are very common. These gifts are not given for our own benefit but for the benefit of the Church. We should not seek these gifts of power, but simply be open to allow the Holy Spirit to use us for his purposes, to build up the Church.

A community of disciples

When I have spoken of a parish as a community of disciples, some people have objected, saying that my view of Church is too limited. They have suggested that people can be active in the Church and do a lot of good things privately, without having to belong to any community. Many don't want to do things with anyone else. They challenge me to deny that they are doing God's work.

Of course God is present in any act of love and good work for others. But that does not mean that that activity has been claimed for Christ to build up his Church. When we refuse to work with one person or another, we refuse to work with Christ in that person. Can we only accept a part of Christ and not accept the whole? A good deed does not build up the Church. It is more likely to build up the person who performs that good deed. Our good deeds should always point to Christ:

> You are the light of the world. A city set on a mountain cannot be hidden. Nor do they light a lamp and then put it under a bushel basket; it is set on a lampstand, where it gives light to all in the house. Just so, your light must shine before others, that they may see your good deeds and glorify your heavenly Father.   MATTHEW 5:14-16

▪ Discipleship is journey

Discipleship is a journey from the cradle to the kingdom. It is a process closely linked both to the stages of our life and the stages of our faith maturity. This journey needs to be understood and appropriately supported at each stage by our Eucharistic community.

As young children, we experience the love of our parents and family. Ideally, we should learn that this love is the presence of God in our lives, whether we recognize him or not. We learn to pass on this love by caring for others.

We begin by taking responsibility for the chores that our parents performed for us— making our beds, keeping our rooms tidy. This also includes caring for ourselves and developing our gifts and talents. It is difficult to love others if we cannot love and care for our self. We also start to care for our family by taking on chores that make their lives easier: washing the dishes, doing the vacuuming. We follow the example of our family by starting to help those around us, through small acts of kindness.

We need to put into practice the values we have learned. It is not enough to pray and obey. As adolescents we are idealistic and believe the world needs to change. If actions are inconsistent with what people say, we distrust them and form new relationships with people we believe we can trust. We need role models whom we can relate to. As young adults we need to live our discipleship in practical ways: feeding the hungry, providing shelter for the homeless, caring for asylum seekers, helping the sick to get around at Lourdes. We also need plenty of social interaction.

When we get married and have babies, that youthful idealistic involvement fades with the setting sun as we face another sleepless night of bottles and diapers and the worry of financial demands to maintain a home and put food on the table. The pressures of time and frequent re-locations (compared to our parents and grandparents) leave us isolated and lonely. Peer pressure, especially through the children, leaves us struggling to choose between our values and keeping up with the Joneses.

We need people we trust to just listen to us and confirm that it's OK to say no to the relentless demands for more, more, more. We need those same people to help us to focus on God in our love, and help us to share him with our children. As we struggle to keep our relationships afloat, sometimes unsuccessfully, we need that shoulder to cry on or the encouragement of a hug and a smile as we keep our head above water for another day. We need to be a family, where we always belong, propping each other up, no matter what.

As the fire of our youth and early adulthood burns down to warming coals, experience often refines our priorities. Mature oaks are not easily blown over by the storms around them. We may become more certain in our faith because life may have shown us just how close God is to us in every crisis, when we choose to look out for him. Possessions and things matter less. Love matters more. We choose more carefully how we use our time and understand that, minute by minute, we can lay down our lives for our friends. In this situation, we find ways to help others more and more, even if it is not in the context of a parish. Given the opportunity, we like to get involved in passing on the love of God to others.

In our old age humility is often thrust upon us, even if we are not yet ready for it. Our opinions count for little and our labor becomes feeble. We become dependent upon others sometimes for even the most basic quality of life. We are emptied of all the things in this life that prop us up. Our self-sufficiency is eroded. It is much easier to give than to receive. We may have spent a lifetime giving to others. Now we have to learn to receive and allow others to serve us. All we have left to give is a generous smile of gratitude and a blessing for those who serve us, however inadequate their efforts may be.

And so our life cycle naturally directs us toward love, to get ready for the ultimate Holy Communion of the kingdom. With humility and love for one another, our whole life becomes an experience of Christ's joy.

> "This is how all will know that you are my disciples, if you have love for one another." JOHN 13:35

TEN

The family of God

God created [humankind] in his image; in the divine image he created [humankind]; male and female he created them. God blessed them, saying to them: "Be fertile and multiply; fill the earth and subdue it."

GENESIS 1:27-28

God is a Trinitarian, creative relationship of love. That is the image and likeness we are created to be. The prime, but not exclusive, creative relationship of love is the family. As the family of God, the Church is also the creative relationship of love that builds on our first experiences of love in our families, to guide and support us to love one another as Jesus loves us.

The symbiotic relationship between the family and parish needs to be understood and nurtured. Families are the place we should learn to love those who love us. The parish should help us to learn to love those who don't love us. This is how we learn to become love as God is love, so that we can become one with God. Unless this relationship is recognized and steps are taken in the parish to actively address both spiritual and practical needs of families in a focused way, the decline of Christ-centered family values and the Church itself will both continue.

Before we can love others unconditionally, as God does, most of us need to have first experienced unconditional love ourselves. Before we explore how parishes can reach and support families to live a life in Christ, we should understand what makes a family effective, because the family, despite all its messiness, is recognized as the domestic church:

> From the wedlock of Christians there comes the family, in which new citizens of human society are born, who by the grace of the Holy Spirit received in baptism are made children of God, thus perpetuating the people of God through the centuries. The family is, so to speak, the domestic church.   *LUMEN GENTIUM, #11*

It is unfortunate that when we speak about the need for strong, loving families today, people often assume that we mean the nuclear family of mom, dad and 2.75 children. This is an inaccurate exclusive image that does not reflect the reality of families as we live in them today.

> If the symbol of domestic church appears to be exclusive and to absolutize the nuclear family...it is not because the concept itself is limiting, but rather because Anglo culture has too restricted an appreciation of family. When faith and culture are more intertwined, and when family is understood to have more extended, flexible boundaries, the church and home need not be antithetical.
>   BOURG, 2004: 14

Family means that network of relationships within which we are most likely to experience and come to appreciate the necessity of unconditional love. In Africa, it is said that it takes a village to bring up a child. A child raised in a family that is part of a wider, caring community is more likely to accept the responsibilities of freedom and be more able to embark on that journey of becoming love, than one who is raised to believe that individual rights take precedence over all else. In a society where the extended family no longer meaningfully exists, the parish needs to be that caring community of love.

What does the "domestic Church" look like?

> At different moments in the Church's history and also in the Second Vatican Council, the family has well deserved the beautiful name of "domestic Church." This means that there should be found in every Christian family the various aspects of the entire Church. Furthermore, the family, like the Church, ought to be a place where the Gospel is transmitted and from which the Gospel radiates.
>
> *EVANGELII NUNTIANDI*, 71

■ The five key purposes of Church apply equally to the domestic Church

The first key practice is to strive to have a common purpose in the family. If we accept that our purpose as humankind is to learn to become love so that we can become one with God, then a family should strive to be in a Holy Communion with God and each other. The first step to communion is for a family to recognize and affirm in a conscious way that God is the love, the glue that binds our relationships together. This recognition and affirmation places him at the core of everything we value most in our lives.

In doing this, families will comply with Jesus' instruction: "You shall love the Lord your God with all your heart, with all your soul, and with all your mind" (Mt 22:37).

The second key practice is to be a family. This involves being tolerant and accepting of one another and going out of your way to make each member feel welcome and included. Family is the place most likely to welcome you, especially when nobody else wants you. Family reflects the intended welcoming communion of the Church that is promised through baptism: "baptizing them in the name of the Father, and of the Son, and of the holy Spirit" (Mt 28:19).

The third key practice is formation, through which we learn and teach each other to become the person God intended us each to be. This includes but goes beyond training and education to listening, sharing family history and identity, guidance, and sharing life and faith experiences. Through this process we should also discover and value each other's gifts and talents and learn how to use them, individually and collaboratively, to keep Christ's commandments. This follows Christ's teaching: "and teaching them to observe all that I have commanded you" (Mt 28:20).

The fourth key practice is to use our gifts and talents for the good of all creation. In the first instance this includes chores, recycling, and caring for one another as well as bringing home the bacon to meet the needs of the family. In committing to care for those who love us, we become open to the concept of serving those who don't know, let alone love, us.

Unconditional love is not always romantic, as anyone washing the party dishes when the rest of the family has gone to bed will tell you. It always involves time, effort, tolerance, forgiveness, and acceptance—in other words, a sacrifice of some sort. Ironically, it is through this sacrifice of self-giving that we come to experience Christ's joy in us, as he promised. In this way, we learn to become love and carry out Christ's commandment: "You shall love your neighbor as yourself" (Mt 22:39).

The fifth key practice is to share what we have, including the good news that we are all created only to love and be loved by God and one another. We are all called to proclaim the gospel, and parents have the prime responsibility for sharing the good news with their children. By sharing the good news we fulfill Christ's instruction: "Go, therefore, and make disciples of all nations" (Mt 28:19).

Initially, most families would probably consider these five purposes to be unrealistic because human love tends to be conditional upon the other person loving us. Fear, the opposite of love, always undermines our relationships. We fear that the other person does not love us as much as we love them, and so we hold back. We tell lies to protect our perceived vulnerabilities. Too often our gifts of love come with an invoice attached, and we struggle to forget the list of collected IOUs that we keep in the ledgers that determine the value of our relationships.

> ...domestic churches are characteristically caught up in the tension between ideal and actual, between the attractiveness of their life's goals and the mediocrity of their journey toward those goals. BOURG, 2004: 52

The Church needs families but families need the Church to help them to become strong, so that they may better fulfill their commission from Christ to the apostolate.

> The lay apostolate...is a participation in the salvific mission of the Church itself. Through their baptism and confirmation all are commissioned to that apostolate by the Lord Himself. *LUMEN GENTIUM*, 33

When people view religion as being hypocritical and lacking in spirituality, it is probably because they have never experienced the love that we profess. However, we can show this love to them by helping them to understand that their love is deeply spiritual because it is the presence of God, whether they recognize and accept it or not.

So many people have broken, messy families. Life is often a struggle, and they have nobody who will take the time to help and encourage them or just provide a shoulder to cry on. Loneliness and isolation have become major issues in the world we live in.

In 1972, Fr. Peter McGrath, CP, developed a practical approach for parishes to become a family to each other, based upon Jesus' commandment to love one another as he loves us:

> With loneliness and isolation so prevalent in our so-ciety, there is a genuine need for people to know and support each other. Family Groups create an extended family atmosphere within the community and are open to everyone. Our focus is on people caring for, loving and accepting each other.
>
> THE PASSIONIST FAMILY GROUP MOVEMENT

The idea is that parishioners form groups of around eight to sixteen families who become a family to one another. Everyone is welcome to participate, irrespective of the shape of their family, or even lack of family. (This example of a society driven by knowl-edge and practice of Jesus' love has influenced and been valued by the rest of society, as evidenced by the fact that in 2011, Fr. McGrath was awarded the Medal of Order of Australia "for his services to the community through the Catholic Church.")

A major benefit of this approach is that there is no demand on already overworked priests to make this happen. Families do it themselves. It requires two or three key people to coordinate the parish groups, and the groups themselves decide how best to be a family together. Each family group needs a leader and a backup to connect with the parish coordinators, but responsibility for making things happen is shared by all members of the group. The underlying motivation that distinguishes family groups from any other social group is to fulfill Jesus' commandment to "love one another as I have loved you."

Practical support naturally follows as families come together in their groups, once a month. These are low-cost or no-cost gatherings in one another's homes or wherever the group decides to meet. Each family brings food and refreshments to share. Trust and relationships grow from simple interactions and conversations until all become family to one another and live the values we want for our children, always driven by the commandment to "love one another as I have loved you." The level of support for each other naturally increases, the more we care for one another. As in all families, some members will be close and involved while others will drift around the periphery, perhaps joining only at high days and holidays.

Family groups would be supported by periodic talks and discussions to recognize the presence of God in our everyday lives and to engage with him. Examples of talks are:

- The Sermon on the Mount and the discourse at the Last Supper
- Sharing experiences of how a family becomes conscious that God is always present, as the love in our relationships
- Periodic catechesis
- Sharing ways of praying, including the silence of contemplative prayer and *lectio divina*

As the family group matures, it is likely that practicing Christ's commandment will lead them to find ways to reach out to help others. Examples are:

- Providing respite care to members who may be caring for a parent suffering from dementia
- Having a social for the senior citizens in the community
- Becoming more involved in small ministry groups described in the next chapter

Active caring family groups are far more likely to become active volunteers in ways that benefit the parish, schools, the wider community, and society in general.

A significant advantage of forming family groups is that we reinforce connectedness across the generations. Family remains across all age groups, and family groups can effectively retain the connection across the entire cycle of life.

Family groups can more easily

- Keep young children close, involved, listening, learning, and safe
- Help arrange the practical, caring service activities that give meaning to faith for teenagers
- Support young adults to be good role models of positive leadership for younger children
- Be visible examples of simple but powerful love in action
- Help children to benefit from the experience and wisdom of older members
- Arrange support, company and entertainment for older members

People who might otherwise not want to get involved in the parish often enjoy belonging to a family group. It is a great way to help newcomers to town to settle in and make good friends fairly quickly. It is an especially good way of involving young parents living busy lives, who are at that stage where their greatest responsibility is to raise and pass on the faith to their children. Belonging to a family group can be a source of good, common-sense advice and also provide shared confidence in childrearing.

ELEVEN

Small ministry groups

Family groups will help to sustain people in their faith, share it with their children, and care for others, especially in those crucial years of young parenthood. But the parish and the wider community have needs that require more organization, focus, and perhaps even time, which will not always be found in family groups.

■ Small ministry groups

From earliest times, members of the Church have come together in small groups to pray, learn, serve, and share the good news together. As parishes get bigger, in these days of parish closures, clustering, and mergers, people are finding small groups an excellent way of being Church. This is no accident. The Church grows when the laity is active, and small groups are best for enabling an active laity. Everyone in the parish is invited and encouraged to join a small ministry group within which people pray, learn, serve, share the gospel, and build community together. This operates in harmony with and does not compete with family groups.

The emphasis in family groups is on building close, trusted relationships to support one another first. This naturally encourages those who benefit from this loving care to want to pass on God's love to others. It is quite common for family groups to engage in activities that reach out to others, often in ad hoc, informal ways, although this is not always so. However, unless all the members of a family group have complementary gifts and talents in ministering to others, some may be left out or their efforts may be less effective than they might desire.

Small ministry groups each have a different ministry, which depends upon the complementary gifts and talents of the members of that group. Accountants and bakers may easily belong to the same family group, but it is unlikely that a baker would be interested in the financial affairs of the parish, or that accountants would be passionate about baking the best apple pies this side of creation for the confirmation party.

Membership of each small ministry group should be open to all who have the required gifts and talents to exercise that group's ministry. Every small ministry group has similar objectives, all of which are firmly embedded in the five pastoral purposes:

WORSHIP

- To ensure that we seek Holy Communion with the Holy Spirit and each other through communal and private prayer and the Holy Eucharist so that we remain firmly focused as a group on working to bring about the reign of God. Every meeting opens with an invitation to the Holy Spirit to guide our efforts and closes with a prayer of thanks and for the needs of the group and those around us.

WISDOM

- To learn to love one another as Jesus loves us, i.e., growing in Christ together. The group will routinely practice *lectio divina* (contemplative reading of the Scriptures), continually seeking to understand how discipleship—a life in Christ—relates to our life and our work. From time to time the group will participate in programs or use other appropriate resources to explore our faith, e.g., Whole Community Catechesis. The group will also give witness and share faith appropriately with one another, to affirm and gain confidence in our personal faith experiences.
- To continue to improve the capability of the group for their ministry. Initially, there will be parish-specific basic training on Small Ministry Groups, explaining how Small Ministry Groups operate and how these fit into the overall parish structure and ways of working, e.g., health and safety, confidentiality, obtaining funding, roles and responsibilities, meeting structures, annual progress reviews, etc. Where necessary the group will arrange for ministry-specific training as a group or for specific members where appropriate.

WELCOME

- To remain always in Holy Communion with the rest of the parish, especially through regular celebration of the Holy Eucharist as source and summit of our faith.
- To welcome all who are called to use their gifts and talents in the specific ministry of the group, and to ensure that every effort is made to resist moves to become an exclusive club for select members. The group will strive to

build a trusted community through fellowship, socializing, faith sharing, and supporting one another.

- To ensure that they remain part of the wider community of the parish through effective communication and cooperation, and actively participate in parish-wide social and community events.

WELFARE

- To carry out the specific ministry of the group to serve Christ incarnate in our neighbor. This is recognized as laying down our life for our friends, minute by minute in service, as Christ did for us.

- To ensure that everyone clearly understands the specific role (or ministry) of the group and is committed to working with and supporting one another to achieve the objectives of that ministry in the best way possible.

- To ensure that they remain alert to the effectiveness and possible unintended consequences of their efforts and remain ready to continue to learn from experience and adjust their efforts to improve.

WORD

- To make a conscious effort to be aware of their responsibility to invite people to become disciples for Christ and so strive to ensure that the way the group functions always points to a life in Christ as the Way, the Truth, and the Life, so that "our light shines in the sight of people so that, seeing our good works, they may give praise to our Father in heaven" (Mt 5:16, NJB).

- To be ready at all times to accept offers of help and indeed invite people to help us in our work so that they too may begin to experience a life in Christ and come to know him.

The group will meet as often as they consider it to be necessary, but not less than once a month. The format of the meeting is set out in Chapter Thirteen.

◼ Groups and communities

Why do I use the term "Small Ministry Group" rather than "Small Christian Community"?

The word "small" is obvious. These groups should be of a size that allows good trusting relationships to form between all the members, and it should function effectively with the absolute minimum of management bureaucracy. Once you start going beyond twelve to fifteen people, the group loses its intimacy.

The word "ministry" is intended to emphasize that the group has been formed to pass on God's love to others. It is the vehicle through which its members live the action of love by using their gifts and talents to serve others.

In *Good Things Happen* (Westley, 1992), author Dick Westley explains the three differences between a *group* and a *community* and why a community cannot be formed but rather happens.

The first difference is that a group typically is formed to serve its own members, while a community focuses on serving others. Initially many people in a parish lack the confidence or doubt the value of their skills and capabilities to serve others. They join the group to learn and grow in faith together. The first objective of the group is to help its own members so that they can come to help and serve others. We can only love others as much as we love our self. The stronger we become in love and capability and as our confidence grows in our faith, the Holy Spirit, and each other, the more effective we become in serving others.

The second difference is that a community is fully conscious of the presence of the Holy Spirit in all that they do. Groups tend to rely on their own efforts. That conscious awareness of the Holy Spirit comes over time and is dependent upon the willingness of the group to accept their own inadequacies and trust that through the Holy Spirit they can indeed accomplish great things. This is not something that can be decided in a meeting. It is something that happens over time as the relationship between the members and with the Holy Spirit becomes a holy communion.

The third difference is the level of commitment of members to the group or community. When people join for what they can get out of it, they remain committed for as long as they are benefiting personally. In a community, members remain fully committed for as long as they have something to offer others outside of their membership.

Obviously a group can and hopefully will become a community over time, but it is something that happens to them as a result of their prayer, behavior, attitude, and communal relationship. It is not something that can be made to happen as a result of some process or executive decision to call it a community rather than a group.

Calling it a group will not prevent it from becoming a strong community.

■ Identifying gifts and talents

We all have both natural and spiritual gifts and talents, which provide the parish with a rich potential capability. Does your parish know what your gifts are? Has it ever asked? Would you be comfortable having your gifts known, and perhaps even kept on a parish list? (Obviously, this information should be properly controlled and accessed only by those authorized to do so.)

A parish should also respect where people are on their journey and not have unreasonable expectations of them. Before he was married, my son was very involved in youth ministry and used his gifts in that area to the full, which earned him a reputation for getting things done. This reputation preceded him after he got married, and in no time at all he was on the parish council in his new parish, responsible for youth ministry. This commitment demanded up to three nights a week, which was having a distinct negative impact on his responsibilities as a father and husband. He felt torn and guilty at resenting the time taken up with parish work. He and the parish council needed to be reminded that he was at a stage in his journey where his priority was to care for his family and teach his children about love and pass on the faith to them. There was no reason for him to feel guilty about not being able to give as much time to parish work.

■ Existing ministry groups

Before rushing in to do things in a whole new way, it is very important to recognize what is already taking place within the parish. Some small ministry groups that may already exist are the parish council, the ministers of Communion, the lectors/readers/proclaimers, the church cleaners and flower arrangers, the welcomers, the visitors to the sick, the parish life committee, the fundraising committee, the St. Vincent de Paul group, etc.

As part of the new focus on Small Ministry Groups, care should be taken to ensure that existing groups are not made to feel that their efforts are not recognized. Before starting new groups it may be helpful to explore whether existing groups feel that a bit of support and encouragement may attract new members and help them become more invigorated. This should obviously be handled with sensitivity. Any attempt to "fix what ain't broke" can have very negative consequences and undermine the enthusiasm of people who are already doing a very good job. Take the time to explain to them what the new approach to Small Ministry Groups is, and let them decide whether they want to consider following what may be a new format of including faith development, fellowship, prayer, ministry, and mission in their approach to their work. (You may be both encouraged and affirmed to find that these groups are already working this way!)

▨ Assess how balanced the ministries of your parish are

One of the reasons why your parish may not be growing steadily is that the balance of the five pastoral purposes may be somewhat off-kilter. To assess whether this is the case, write the name of each of the ministries of the parish separately on a small Post-it note. Then take five sheets of paper and write one of the following purposes on each: WORSHIP, WELCOME, WISDOM, WELFARE, WORD. Now stick each Post-it note on the page that best reflects the pastoral purpose it relates to.

All ongoing ministries that relate to the Mass, prayer, praise, and worship should be placed on the WORSHIP page. All ongoing ministries that relate to the sacraments of Initiation (baptism, reconciliation, First Communion, confirmation, RCIA), parish social—but not fundraising—events, hospitality, and any other welcoming effort should be placed on the WELCOME page. All ongoing ministries that relate to lifelong formation, Bible study, skills and capability development, intergenerational faith development, retreats, youth and adult catechesis, and formal studies should be placed on the WISDOM page. All ongoing ministries that relate to care of others within the parish and the wider community, such as the poor, prisoners, justice and peace, marriage care, administration, finance, fundraising, the sick and homebound, neighborhood, and asylum seekers, should be placed on the WELFARE page.

While it is recognized that all ministries proclaim the gospel by their example, all ongoing ministries that exist specifically for evangelization, such as street ministry, parents of First Communicants, and seeker teams, should be placed on the WORD page.

When the job is done, have a look at how well balanced your ministries are across the five purposes, and consider whether this analysis may suggest any obvious areas to address for building up your parish.

◼ Potential small ministry groups

I was nervous about giving examples of Small Ministry Groups because a small parish may feel that only a larger parish is equipped to function this way. This is not so. Some parishes have started this approach with only one Small Ministry Group. Start small, rely on the Spirit's guidance, and see what new groups suggest themselves.

In that light please see the following list of possible groups simply as an *aide memoire* to stimulate ideas for the possible next group that you decide to form in your parish.

WORSHIP the Lord

Liturgy preparation, music, choir, lectors, Communion ministers, cleaners and flower arrangers, altar servers, prayer groups, art and environment, audio/visual technologists, Eucharistic adoration, passion play, sacristan, sign language, teen/young adult liturgy, youth choir, charismatic prayer group, Marian ministry, etc.

WELCOME into communion

Welcome ministry, hospitality, teas and coffees, funeral catering, welcome desk, parish social, RCIA, baptism and reconciliation, confirmation, new parish members, nursery, pre-catechumenate, transportation ministry, etc.

Grow in WISDOM

Formation in faith, Bible study, facilitators of new groups, gift discernment, catechesis, retreats, Engaged Encounter, Marriage Encounter, annulment support, mini-retreats, marriage preparation, common-sense parenting, mentor families, men's ministry, women's ministry, etc.

WELFARE of others

Saint Vincent de Paul Society, parish pastoral council, Legion of Mary, the sick, asylum seekers, homeless, street ministry, young moms, singles, divorced and separated, people in business, parish administration, fundraising (including collections), substance abuse, marriage support, neighborhood ministry, Faith Alive Catechesis, bereavement, homebound, funeral rites ministry, job support, Alcoholics Anonymous, Al-Anon, other 12-step groups, blood drives, disability awareness, dementia family support, exercise programs, justice and peace, respect life, chaperones for youth events, youth peer ministry, companion ministry, help for the aged, Women In Need Group Support, ethical business, holiday sharing, drama support, etc.

Proclaiming the WORD

Family mission, parents of first communicants and first reconciliation, parents of confirmation candidates, New Age seekers (guiding them to real spirituality—the Holy Spirit), seekers, Word at Work, Honeymooners, F.L.A.M.E., spiritual companioning, university ministry, Couples for Christ, Landings, book and gift store, homilies on tape, parish mission, Pathways (For Singles), Rising from Divorce, TV & radio ministry, couples nights out, evenings of romance, Couples for Christ, etc.

TWELVE

Key small ministry groups

A few key small ministry groups need to be in place and functioning well so that you have a strong foundation to underpin your mission-driven efforts to build up the parish in the other small ministry groups. The key groups are Social, Hospitality, Liturgy, and Facilitation. It does not mean that other groups cannot function without these groups, but all efforts at effective mission in the parish could be undermined without these groups or if they do not function in a coordinated, mission-driven way.

■ Social small ministry group

A few years ago a parish priest told me of a survey he had seen where people chosen at random in the street were asked what their perceptions of Catholics were. I was horrified at the misconceptions that exist. Their perceptions were that Catholics are against sex, against abortion, against condoms, against divorce; are Irish; promote pedophilia; are against the Bible; aren't Christian; worship the pope. Beyond this prejudiced view, there was little else in their understanding of Catholics.

Clearly we are failing to get across to the secular society the message that Catholics are pro-life, pro-fidelity, pro-responsibility, pro-pastoral care, pro-child safety, universal, driven by the Word of God, and we live to bring about the kingdom of God through our Lord Jesus Christ.

We preach best by example, and one of the most effective ways of exposing others to our example is by making the parish a communal center for the entire surrounding community. One of the easiest ways to involve the surrounding community in our parish life is through our social functions.

All too often in a parish, the word "social" is a synonym for fundraising. Social events that exist purely to raise money tend to exclude anyone who is living on a tight budget, and the social life of the parish ends up as an exclusive club of a limited number of parishioners. When it is obvious that social events are arranged purely as fundraisers, the surrounding community sees no reason to join in to support a church of which their perceptions are already poor.

When the Social Small Ministry Group arranges events that bring people together to eat, drink, dance, and socialize for no other reason than to get to know one another as trusted friends, then the surrounding community will be inclined to come and join in. The cost of tickets should never be more than is enough to cover the costs of the event, and events should be planned to be as inclusive as possible.

However, the social life of the parish should never be mistaken for just another secular social club. It is a key part of building community in the Church and can be a very effective means of helping to fulfill our mission. Everyone should be happy to acknowledge their faith without foisting it on others. Say grace collectively before meals. Offer to pray for anyone who you hear may be having a hard time or suffering from an illness. Offer help to people as you would to a friend. Never be embarrassed or shy to talk about your faith if you are questioned, but keep your comments to answering the question, and concentrate on listening to understand where people are and what their situation is. Keep things light and social, and let them set the pace of faith exploration.

When each event ends, have a prayer—perhaps a collective "Our Father"—and give thanks for the fun and the joy of getting to know one another to build good relationships and a strong community for all.

Not only is the parish social life beneficial for mission, it also helps people who have relocated into the parish to find their way around and make friends with people who have similar values. A strong social community will help to keep new members of the Church more involved and active. An active parish social life for young adults has also been known to lead to good marriages within which faith is more likely to be passed on to children.

The whole community becomes stronger and more caring and supportive of one another, the parish, and the surrounding community when they build positive relationships from mixing socially. Jesus knew what he was doing at the wedding feast at Cana.

■ Hospitality small ministry group

As a stranger visiting a parish for the first time, how welcome do you feel when you walk in the front door and someone greets you with "Would you like to buy a raffle ticket?" Do you feel a bit embarrassed when you decline because you only have the bill that you were going to put into the collection basket? What frame of mind do these thoughts create in you as you prepare for Mass?

Perhaps as Catholics we have become immune to this practice, but what impression of the Church would a seeker get if they were coming for the first time to find out what we are all about? Is this hospitality?

If your extended family and friends were coming around to your home for a celebration, would you not greet them all at the front door when they arrived? You would make sure they had a seat and any items they needed to participate fully. If a long-lost cousin who does not know anybody arrives, we would introduce that person to someone who could be trusted to show them around and make them feel welcome and included. If we suspect that they are unfamiliar with the format of the celebration, we would seat them with someone able to show them what is going on, if need be.

Children would be especially welcome, and we would ensure that they can enjoy the celebration in a way that is meaningful to them. Moms and dads with babies would have a place to change diapers and, if necessary, feed them. After the formal celebration we would make sure that everyone had some refreshment and an opportunity to catch up with one another.

If someone falls ill during the celebration, we rush to help them. We encourage our cousin who is nursing Uncle Albert, who has dementia, to bring him along as well. Knowing how she struggles with him, we might identify someone who is suitably trained to help care for Uncle Albert, so our cousin can have some respite during the celebration.

The Mass is the fullest celebration of our Christianity. You cannot be a Christian alone. To fully celebrate the Mass, we have to be in holy communion with Christ and one another. It is everything any loving family would expect at their most important celebrations and more: greetings, participation, family stories, news, eating, drinking, singing, music, repentance, forgiveness, offering, sacrifice, thanksgiving, sharing, tolerance, acceptance, joy, laughter, helping, loving, all with Christ himself at the center, in us, around us. It is life being lived to the fullest.

The hospitality small ministry group needs to ensure that everyone is properly welcomed and enabled to fully participate in the most joyful celebration and greatest sacrament of our faith.

▪ Liturgy small ministry group

Worship plays a very important part in our missionary efforts, and of course our most important form of worship is the Mass. Once, as I was leaving Mass, someone commented to me that she loved going to Mass when it was celebrated by that particular priest. "He celebrates Mass like he really means it!" I knew exactly what she meant.

Sadly, I have attended more Masses than I care to remember where a stranger may easily consider our greatest form of worship to be devoid of any spirituality at all. We are all human, and even the most sincere priest is going to have days when he goes through the motions. Without sustained conscious effort by all in the Church, it is easy to fall into a habit of celebrating Mass as a well-practiced, familiar ritual where worship is very much between "God and me," rather than in holy communion between Christ and one another. When Mass is celebrated in this way, it is very difficult to find the inspiration we need to go out and serve our neighbor and proclaim the good news.

Remember that the priest alone cannot ensure a great celebration. It also depends on a well-informed and actively participating congregation. The Mass is about the whole Church. In these days where increasingly the parish priest is responsible for more than one community, the quality of worship will suffer if he does not establish a liturgy group to support him in each community. The liturgy groups will do much of the coordination with other involved groups to ensure great celebrations of the Holy Eucharist.

Good preaching is critical to effective mission. Relating Scripture to daily life and the reality of our world is the key to a good homily. It is said that the difference between a good homily and a poor one is about eighteen hours of preparation. This is obviously a significant amount of effort, but a parish priest could benefit enormously if he were to participate in weekly *lectio divina* with members of the liturgy group, where they actively relate the Scripture to their daily lives. He can obtain great insight into the meaning of the Scriptures in our day-to-day lives and gain good ideas to assist him in the preparation of his homily.

The liturgy group should also work closely with the musicians and choir to ensure that the music is relevant to the planned style of worship for any celebration. They should support the music and choral ministries to ensure that new hymns are practiced and that the quality of singing is very good before hymns are sung in any Mass. Too often the congregation does not know the hymn, the singing is appalling, or everything is left to the choir. The primary purpose of the choir is to draw the congregation into participating in the singing.

A good liturgy group will routinely take time to step back and think about ways to make the liturgy more effective for mission. It is tempting to ensure a style of service that is appealing to the people in the pews. There may even be a financial incentive to do so in that some people have been known to give less if the style of service does not appeal to them. However, this can be very shortsighted if the average member of the congregation is over fifty years of age and getting older. They are a naturally shrinking community. I cannot emphasize enough the importance of concentrating on a style of service that will appeal to families and young people. If we don't focus on families and youth, we are ignoring the people who most obviously need to hear the good news, if it is to be passed on.

Jesus was quite clear about the place of children in the Church:

> At this time the disciples came to Jesus and said, "Who is the greatest in the kingdom of Heaven?" So he called a little child to him whom he set among them. Then he said, "In truth I tell you, unless you change and become like little children you will never enter the kingdom of Heaven. And so, the one who makes himself as little as this little child is the greatest in the kingdom of Heaven."
>
> MATTHEW 18:1-4 [NJB]

If we want young people, remove the existing barriers. Sing songs that they enjoy. Use musical instruments that appeal to them. Give homilies that relate to the issues in their lives. Invite them to participate in everything. Teach them how to love by being the love we want them to be. Be generous in our giving and acceptance and open-mindedness. People learn by example.

I repeat what I said earlier. I have often heard it said that there is no point in having a style of service that focuses on children because no children attend Mass in the parish. If you want something, behave as if you already have it. Families and young people will not come to a place that has little meaning for them.

■ Facilitators small ministry group

When small ministry groups are formed, they need help and guidance to become effective in terms of ongoing growth in faith, catechesis, interaction with the rest of the parish, and ever-improving capability. Without a common understanding and inclusive approach to small group ministry, there is a real risk that small groups can quickly become exclusive and perhaps even elitist clubs. The ministry of facilitation of small ministry groups would be to help form and guide other small ministry groups to ensure that they become as effective as possible and remain aligned and in full communion with the rest of the parish.

This group would also be responsible for helping existing groups to become more effective in all aspects of their ministry and becoming active disciples. They would ensure that each group has a clear role and defined responsibilities, to avoid overlap, confusion, and conflict with other groups.

This team will also identify new opportunities for service to others and will invite parish members to form new groups. This group will also be the first port of call for anyone who recognizes a need that the parish could potentially meet.

In effect, this is an internal "evangelization" team whose role is to encourage existing members of the parish to become more active. At the same time, however, it is important to note that its purpose is strictly to guide, facilitate, and empower.

No group is more important than any other. The reason for emphasizing these groups is purely practical, as they put in place the means to more easily promote and effectively implement small ministry groups, as a means of engaging the laity in accepting co-responsibility for the apostolate and building up the body of Christ.

THIRTEEN

Small ministry groups meetings

Every Small Ministry Group in the parish should share a common structure, if this kind of approach to being Church is to be effective. If every group is free to do its own thing, it won't be long before they are competing with one another and becoming exclusive clubs. It is very important that all Small Ministry Group meetings engage with all five pastoral purposes and remain fully in communion with the rest of the parish.

We have developed a twelve-step structure, adapted from the Lumko Method (Catholic Biblical Federation, 2002), which seems to work very well in achieving these objectives. Previously established groups that have decided to follow this approach have commented that their meetings are calmer, better focused, and more productive with fewer disagreements—and they don't seem to take any longer.

Ensure that there is a facilitator for each meeting and that everyone brings a copy of the Bible. It does not matter if the translations differ—in fact, such differences can be enriching when they are shared.

Here are the twelve steps:

■ Invite the Lord

The facilitator invites everyone to sit down, relax, and put all their cares, concerns, and distractions aside. He or she asks someone to invite the Holy Spirit to join the meeting and to guide and inspire it. A moment of silence follows, to allow everyone to focus on the presence of the Lord in their midst, greet him quietly, and just enjoy his presence in companionable silence.

■ Scripture reading

The facilitator asks the members to open their Bible to the chosen text. It may be a randomly selected passage, or the group may choose to read the entire Bible in a structured way from meeting to meeting. Most commonly, the gospel of the next Sunday is chosen for reflection. It is important that texts should not be chosen to support a particular agenda. Once everyone has found the text and settled down, the facilitator announces the verses to be read and invites someone to read the passage slowly and clearly.

■ Immersion in the reading

After the text has been read, all remain silent, reflecting on words or phrases that resonate with them in some way. After some moments, the facilitator invites everyone to repeat those words or phrases, without any other comment. Members should simply repeat the word or phrase. After each person has spoken, the next person should wait long enough before speaking to allow everyone to repeat the word or phrase three or four times to embrace and absorb it. In this way all can immerse themselves ever deeper in the reading.

▨ Relating the reading to our lives

When the group again becomes silent, the facilitator invites another person, ideally of the opposite sex to the previous reader, to read the full text again, slowly and clearly. When the reading is complete, the facilitator calls for silence to reflect on what the reading is saying to each person in the context of their life, work, and ministry. Allow a fixed period for this, say three minutes. After the reflection, the facilitator will ask everyone to share their reactions. This is a very powerful and effective form of catechesis—sharing our faith with one another. It powerfully affirms the reality of our own experience of Christ and engenders confidence to go out and give witness and share the good news. It also builds trust, tolerance, acceptance, understanding, friendship, and love within the group.

▨ The work we are called to do

The group is now ready to get down to the practical aspects of their ministry in a more calm, tolerant, and focused frame of mind. The facilitator asks the group to search for Christ in the needs that have been placed before the group, and leads the group through those needs in an ordered way:

- First, they will review progress on actions allocated at the previous meeting.
- Where actions are completed, they will be closed. Where actions are unfinished, the group will review whether it is on track or if there are any obstacles to be overcome.
- Actions to resolve obstacles will be identified.
- If any unfinished action is no longer relevant, it will be closed.
- Lessons from any experience gained will be identified.

This should not be viewed in a narrow way that simply considers a successful result to the action, but more broadly—how have people, including the people doing the work, benefited from the experience, and how has the love of God been shared?

- The group will consider what can be learned—both positive and what needs to be improved—from things that never worked as well as they could have. They will then consider what could be learned from their successes.
- Actions will be identified to ensure that the learning is achieved and applied—most especially in terms of improving our sharing the love of God.
- Next they will consider new needs that have been identified. The needs will be explained. Possible solutions will be identified.

■ Discerning our group priorities

It is not possible realistically to resolve every problem we may come across. There is only so much each group is equipped to do. Wisdom requires us to acknowledge our strengths and weaknesses. There are only so many hours in the day. We don't always have the needed gifts and talents. Resources may be limited. The group should only take on work that it can achieve by realistically stretching itself. God calls us to come out of our comfort zones, but he does not expect us to destroy our motivation by setting ourselves up for failure. For those tasks that the group is unable to do, consider whether another group within the parish may be able to assist to get the task done, or you may consider working ecumenically with another church in the area.

■ Allocating our work

Having decided what work the group will take on, the next step is to identify the activities or actions needed to achieve it. Responsibility for carrying out each action should be allocated to one person only, even if that person has to rely on others to get the job done. If everyone is responsible, no one is responsible, and the job won't get done. Make sure that you keep a record in the minutes of who is doing what and by when.

■ Remaining in communion

Ensure that you keep minutes of your meeting and that a copy is always provided to your group, the ministry group of facilitators, and any other groups or people your parish organizational procedures dictate. Remember that good communication calls for more than recording something in the minutes or putting it in the parish newsletter. Such forms of communication are passive, relying on people being motivated to read them. If there is something that another group or person needs to know, meet and discuss it, send an email, a text, or get on the phone. In your meeting identify who else needs to know what is going on about any issue, and allocate someone to ensure that they're informed.

■ Arrange approvals

Small ministry groups are not free to do as they please. As part of the parish, they need to abide by parish structures and realities. Many situations will require the approval of the pastor, pastoral or finance council, or other authorized staff or committee members. For example, new needs a group wishes to take on could have financial demands beyond their allocated budget. Actual expenditure will need the pastor's or the financial administrator's personal approval. There may be a need to obtain media publicity or respond to an inquiry from the press. Identify what actions on your plan require approval, and allocate responsibility to a member of the group to obtain such approval.

■ Enjoying fellowship

With the main business of the meeting over, it is time for fellowship. People work best together when they take the time to get to know and trust each other. Eating, drinking, and good conversation are very effective in building strong relationships. Jesus was always eating and drinking with everyone around him. This doesn't have to be elaborate; it could be finger food or perhaps just a cup of coffee and something to nibble.

■ Learning and growing together

Ongoing learning and growing together has already taken place in previous steps. In sharing how the reading relates to our lives, we are exposed to how Christ touches the lives of those around us, and in that understanding we grow in our relationship with him and each other. In exploring the lessons in our work, we learn how to become more effective in our ministry. However, the group is encouraged to do more. One way of doing this may be to have a different member of the group share a small lesson from something they have read or perhaps show a short video of five or ten minutes to stimulate thinking and learning within the group. It is also possible that the group may decide to meet more often and have each alternate meeting concentrate on a formal course in faith or their ministry, while the other meetings concentrate on the work of their ministry.

■ Closing prayer

At the end of the meeting the facilitator asks the group to settle down and be quiet and take a moment of silence to think about the people around them, friends, family, colleagues, and any other people that they are aware of who may be in need of prayer. Then they are invited to share that need for everyone to pray for. After this the facilitator will close the meeting with a prayer that everyone is familiar with and can join in, e.g., The Lord's Prayer.

This meeting structure ensures that the five pastoral purposes, WORSHIP, WELCOME, WISDOM, WELFARE, and WORD, are embedded in our way of working in small ministry groups. Everybody participating fully in a small ministry group will naturally and automatically be functioning in a holistic and balanced, effective Church.

FOURTEEN

Becoming a community of disciples

This is a broad outline on how to become a Community of Disciples. It is intended as a guide, rather than an inflexible methodology. While each stage builds on what has gone before, that does not mean that everything has to be done in a strict sequence. Consider what is most appropriate for your parish and adjust accordingly. Also, before rushing in to start, it's important to take stock of what good things your parish already has in place. Build on what you have, and if something is already working well, support it and help it to become more effective.

This is a very broad-brush outline, giving just enough information to understand what each stage is and how it relates to the other stages. More detail follows after the outline.

1. Start and encourage the whole parish to keep praying: "Here I am, Lord; use me as you will."
   a. If we, the branches, are not firmly connected to the vine, we will bear no fruit.

2. Invite a small group of people to enable the strategy to happen.

    a. They will plan, organize, find the right people to do things, and generally lend a helping hand.

3. Help people to rediscover the purpose of the Holy Eucharist as both source and summit of our faith—the *source* that enables us to love one another as Jesus loves us, which leads us into a Trinitarian holy communion with one another and with God as the love in our relationships—the *summit*.

    a. Run a parish mission or give a series of talks on consecutive Sundays based on John chapters 13—17. This makes it abundantly clear that the Holy Eucharist both empowers us and gives us our greatest call to mission: to carry out Jesus' new commandment, "Love one another as I have loved you." This is the Way, the Truth, and the Life. By loving one another, in unity with Christ—through him, with him, and in him—we become one with each other and God, now and later.

4. At the conclusion of the mission or talks, invite and help members of the parish to form groups of families with one objective, to learn to love one another as Jesus loves us and to become family to each other. A big advantage is that this helps the laity to take on their essential roles in building up the kingdom.

    a. Family groups get the positive energy of the Holy Spirit going in the parish. Faces become names, names become friends, and friends become family. As people look out for one another, as they learn to love one another as Jesus loves us, and as they experience the joy of Christ, they naturally open up to recognize the needs of others and slowly get involved in all aspects of a life in Christ.

5. Give family groups time to get to know one another socially and to build relationships. Then start adult/family catechesis to build confidence in exploring faith together. (Some parishes have chosen to start catechesis before forming family groups. Decide what is most appropriate for your parish.)

    a. We discover Christ by sharing and discussing our personal experiences of Christ with each other. When people begin to respond to our faith-sharing, we gain the confidence to share the good news with others. In a year or two, family groups will be confidently supporting each other as well as parents who are not in family groups to prepare for the sacraments.

6. As family groups start to get off the ground, encourage all existing groups, including the parish council, to begin each meeting with *lectio divina.*

    a. Meetings will be calmer, more focused, and more productive as they start to consider and focus on what the Holy Spirit is calling us to do.

7. Over time, more people become infected with the energy of the Holy Spirit. Arrange an off-site retreat to consider how the parish can be a more effective Church.

    a. Explain the five purposes set out in the Two Great Commandments and the Great Commission.

    b. Consider what ministries would make the parish more effective.

    c. Explain how Small Ministry Groups operate.

    d. Invite people to share their gifts and talents and to fill out a form giving details of what gifts they would like to offer.

    e. Explain what the next steps will be.

8. Form a Small Ministry Group of facilitators who, using the database of gifts and talents, will invite and help people to form Small Ministry Groups where each group has a different ministry.

    a. Ensure that the key ministry groups (discussed earlier) are in place.

    b. Don't try to boil the ocean—boil a kettle at a time. Work with one or two groups to get them properly established before starting more.

9. If you have a parish school, consider evangelizing young parents in the school community when around thirty to forty percent of parishioners are actively involved either in active family or small ministry groups.

    a. Young parents are the people most likely to influence and share the good news with the next generation, and we have a unique opportunity to evangelize by encouraging them to form family groups of families linked to the parish.

10. Sustain this community of disciples by setting in motion the ongoing development cycle linked to the liturgical year, described later in the book.

    a. Building up the Church in the parish is a journey, not an event. It takes time. Each year should be better than the previous year. Identify needs in Advent. Reflect on how needs are being met in Lent. Evaluate how well the celebration of Easter reflects parish life in communion with Christ. Plan to better meet needs after Easter. Commission everyone again at Pentecost.

■ Prayer

Invite the whole parish at every opportunity, especially every Mass, to pray for active discipleship within the parish. Explain what active discipleship means: worshiping and praying together; building community; learning and sharing faith; ever-better pastoral ministry and sharing the good news. Continually invite everyone to make a habit of praying the prayer of commitment: "Here I am, Lord; use me as you will." It's amazing how the Holy Spirit creates real energy in a parish around this prayer.

■ The Mass

We need to meet people where they are on their faith journey. Although they may have regularly attended Mass for most of their lives, many Catholics lack a clear understanding of what the Mass is about. We should meet people where they are and catechize from there. The Mass is our most powerful call to active ministry and mission. Make sure that message is well expressed and understood. Take a good look at the quality of celebration of the Mass, and explore what people actually understand it to mean. Continually strive to make the Mass more participative and meaningful as our call to mission.

The account of the Last Supper in chapters 13 to 17 of John's gospel gives us three very clear messages Jesus wants us to heed:

- Without him we can do nothing. As branches, unless we are connected to the vine, we will not bear fruit. We are not just spiritually connected to Christ. Jesus gave us his body to eat and his blood to drink because he wants us to also be one with him, here on Earth. We are intended to be his body to continue his work and bear abundant fruit. He is the source of all we need to do this.

- His work, which we are to continue, is to share the love of God with all of creation. Three times at the Last Supper (Jn 13:34, Jn 15:12, Jn 15:17), he reminded us of his command to love one another, just as he loves us. This is not a favor he is asking us to carry out for him at our convenience. This is the fulfillment of the purpose of our lives.
- Only by loving one another just as Jesus loves us can we fulfill our purpose to become love, one with God and each other, in a holy communion, now and for all eternity. This is the summit that Jesus prayed for us, to the Father, at the Last Supper.

Loving one another is the way in which even those who have not heard the name of Jesus experience him in their hearts and come to kingdom. While it is possible to become one with God without knowing the name of Jesus, the greatest gift we can give to anyone is to share his good news and the gift that he gave us in the Holy Eucharist, which enables us live the Way, the Truth, and the Life, through him, with him, and in him.

Take the time to prepare for Mass in this context. Make sure the call to discipleship is always clear. Make sure everyone can participate to the fullest extent in this communal celebration of the source and summit of our faith. Never sing a hymn that has not been practiced. The readers should truly proclaim the meaning of the Word through clear, slow, well-prepared reading and diction.

Where there is only one Mass on a Sunday, change the style of the Mass so that each sector of the community has a style that appeals to them in the course of a month. If you are fortunate enough to have more than one Mass on a Sunday, make sure one of the Masses is a fully participative children's Mass. Children are the future of the Church, and if they enjoy Mass, they will encourage their parents to join them. Where children are welcome and enjoy the Mass, they become great catechizers and evangelizers to parents, grandparents, cousins, aunts, and uncles. Children are great activists for Christ! Their love can be so uncomplicated and appealing.

Before the final blessing at the end of every Mass, invite everyone to look and see the hands of Christ in their own and pray: "Lord, please use my heart, feet, hands, and voice to share your love with those around me."

■ Form family groups of families

One of the most meaningful ways we can love one another as Jesus loves us would be to be a real family to one another in the parish. This can be achieved very effectively by forming family groups of families. People understand the concept of family as a network of relationships where you are most likely to experience and come to appreciate the value of unconditional love.

Family groups are not simply another way of being social. They are intended to be family to one another, driven by Jesus' commandment to "love one another as I have loved you." All their interactions and their effectiveness should be driven by this purpose.

Form a small ministry group of enthusiastic individuals, if the Facilitators Small Ministry Group cannot coordinate the family groups as well, and have them explore the Passionist Family Group Movement website at www.pfgm.org to pick up ideas and other useful resources to help them. They should take the lead to initiate and establish family groups and be the coordinating point for guidance and support. They should also make sure the parish priest is kept informed of all family group news and activities. (The beauty of this kind of group formation, though, is that it is lay-run and does not put any additional demands on the pastor's workload.)

At a meeting of those who are interested, the coordinators should first share about the meaning of the Mass, and then briefly explain the concept of being a family to one another, pointing out that we know the faces but perhaps not the names of those with whom we regularly celebrate the Mass. Emphasize that family means more than the nuclear family and that everyone has a place in the parish family, even if they have no family of their own. All are welcome—married, unmarried, divorced, single parents—it does not matter. All that matters is that we are willing to try to follow Christ's commandment to love one another as he loves us.

At the meeting explain the concept of becoming family to one another. Emphasize again that membership is not restricted to nuclear families nor to members of the Catholic Church. Anyone is welcome as long as they are prepared to try to keep Christ's commandment to love one another as he loves us. Explain that each family group will consist of approximately eight to sixteen "families," whatever their makeup may be. The number of families in each group of families will be influenced by the number of children in total.

It is a good idea for families attending the same Mass each week to belong to the same group. They will find that the Mass has a greater sense of a holy communion between each other and with God (even if some are not in communion with the Church). They will also be more willing to help and support families with young children or perhaps support a family that may bring a parent suffering from Alzheimer's. They will be more inclined to participate in sacramental celebrations of their family members.

Ideally each group should have members across the generations from young children to grandparents. As the sense of family grows in each group, there is no reason why new "grandparents" should not help busy parents in the family to prepare their children for the sacraments.

Common sense should always prevail in family groups. While it is much easier for a family group that knows each other well to keep an eye on young children in the family group, parents should always make sure that they know and trust anybody that they might ask to care for their children. They should be just as careful as they are with the parents of their children's friends at school. Family groups can significantly improve the safety of children within their group: not only do they watch over them while in the group, they also see them out and about in daily life, and keep an eye on them there as well.

What happens if one or another member of a family group fails to act in a way that heeds Jesus' commandment? Obviously none of us is perfect; like all families, members will not always get along and sometimes may do silly things. This does not mean that they have excluded themselves. Family bonds are much stronger than that. However, tough love may be necessary when, for example, someone has an uncontrollable addiction that may compromise the safety of others, and it would be inappropriate for that person to participate in any collective family activities or interact with anyone who may be vulnerable. In a situation like that, the family group may refer or try and get support for that person to get their life back on track, just as families try to do, when they cannot deal with a situation themselves.

Family groups meet about once a month to do something that they want to do together. Each group should organize its own activities. The only requirement is that that they start each gathering with a prayer for guidance and support to keep Jesus' commandment to love one another as he loves us. They can meet at a member's home or any other suitable venue for the planned activity. Food and a time to eat together are always a recommended practice. People get to know and trust each other when they chat and eat together, even if the meal is no more than a slice of bread and cheese. These should be low- or no-cost events, with everyone bringing whatever they have available to share, without any attempts to outdo each other.

Three or four times a year there might be a plenary meeting of all groups, arranged by the parish coordinators, where a catechetical topic is presented for discussion by each group. This sort of meeting should last no more than an hour, and be followed by a social of some sort with food, so different groups can share ideas with each other and recognize their place in the wider Family of God.

■ Catechesis

As family groups start maturing, they are going to need more ongoing faith formation than a weekly homily can provide. Typically, I hear three significant objections to this idea:

- The already overworked parish priest does not have the time to do this.
- There is no money to pay for education programs.
- There are no trained catechists, or the catechists don't feel comfortable teaching adults.

Here's the good news. None of this need stop you from starting ongoing lifelong learning in your parish now. Again Jesus showed the way:

> At that moment his disciples returned, and were amazed
> that he was talking with a woman, but still no one said,
> "What are you looking for?" or "Why are you talking with
> her?" The woman left her water jar and went into the town
> and said to the people, "Come see a man who told me ev-
> erything I have done. Could he possibly be the Messiah?"
> They went out of the town and came to him.
>
> JOHN 4:27–30

The first recorded evangelist was the Samaritan woman at the well. She was not a trained catechist. In fact, as a Samaritan she had highlighted the differences between her beliefs and the beliefs of Jews in her earlier discussion with Christ. By her own admission her morals had excluded her from the community of the village she lived in. And yet, she felt compelled to share her experience of Christ with others.

If we are to be successful evangelists and catechizers, as she was, our most powerful message will be our own experience of Christ and how that has changed our lives. By talking about our experiences we draw others to Christ and in the process gain confidence in the validity of our experience. We grow in faith through seeing our impact on others. We learn as we hear about the experience of Christ in the lives of others and relate their experiences to our own lives.

Theological reflection and contemplative reading of the Scriptures don't require trained catechists as facilitators. All you need is a Bible, no matter the translation. This approach is excellent for learning and teaching, and as people develop confidence in their faith, more are likely to want to be trained as catechists.

Don't hesitate to augment your parish-based groups from time to time with formal catechesis programs. These will only add to the strong foundation and understanding of faith that the groups are building. As maturity in faith grows, you may want to consider a formal curriculum of catechesis at the deanery level that you run over a year of two, starting a new course each year. There would be a class every two to four weeks, depending on how quickly you want to get through the curriculum. (A group of parishes working together could help defray the costs of a formal program.)

It may be useful to have a few basic ground rules for catechesis gatherings:

- Catechesis is about sharing our insights into our faith and our personal experiences of Christ, so that we may grow in Christ together.
- We always seek to be guided by the Holy Spirit.
- This is not an opportunity to bash the views of others or any teachings or structures that we may not agree with.
- We listen respectfully to insights and the faith experience of others.
  - » We have one mouth and two ears.
  - » We should listen at least twice before speaking once.
- We consider how other's insights into their faith and experience of Christ relate to our life.
- If we are worried that an expressed view may not be from God, we consider whether it is likely to make people want to love God and each other more, unconditionally and without any sense of being manipulated for any purpose. If it does, then it is from God.

There are a number of themes that are worth exploring, and some themes—e.g., the Old and New Testaments—will take more than one session. Meeting every other week, the program can run from September to June of each year. Consider the following questions to arrive at themes for each session.

- What is exploring and sharing faith about?
- Who is God and why did he make us?
- What is Spirituality really about?
- What has the Bible got to do with life today? Why should we bother reading it?
- Does God answer our prayers? Why does God allow bad things to happen?
- Is Church really relevant today? Is it not enough to be a good person?
- Was Jesus truly human? Is he truly God?
- What is right and wrong, when it seems to change with each generation?
- Are repentance and reconciliation relevant today?
- Why should I be Catholic? After all, people who haven't heard of Jesus can get into heaven.
- Why did Jesus give us the Holy Eucharist?
- What was so important about Vatican II?
- Why would I want to be a disciple of Christ? What does that mean?
- What does "proclaim the gospel" mean? Am I expected to go around knocking on doors?
- What has Catholic social teaching got to do with anything?
- What do you mean we all have a unique vocation? How do I discover mine?

Don't be put off by the broad range of subjects. Rather than a formalized, all-encompassing program, have a short presentation on the theme, given by a facilitator, with a few well-thought-out questions to encourage the conversation. The purpose is not to try and explain everything but rather to start a journey of faith discovery, as a result of which people start thinking and developing their confidence in their ability to discuss and share their experience of faith.

This kind of approach can make those who have not explored their faith much since leaving school very nervous—they may be unsure of being able to discern whether inspiration is from God or not. Skillful guidance by the facilitator to keep everyone focused on the key question of whether the idea expressed helps one to love God and neighbor more should slowly gain the confidence and trust of the tentative ones. When people begin to understand about the nature of unconditional and unselfish love for one another—and how one's own unique gifts contribute to the betterment of all—the invitation to join small ministry groups should be met enthusiastically.

People may join the Church but their loyalty and commitment derive from the relationships that they form with other members of the Church. Ideally everyone should have the opportunity to join a family group or a small ministry group in which to exercise their gifts and talents in service of others and to develop meaningful relationships to journey together to the kingdom.

See Appendix III for an outline of how to present beginning small ministry groups in your parish.

■ Build community

Arrange social and other events to help people belong. Each event needs to reflect the passion of those involved, which will draw others in. Plymouth Diocese in England has a program called "Creative Ways of Being Church." It lists some elements that help to make a gathering successful:

Create opportunities for people to:
- Tell a story or visit nostalgia
- Laugh and make friends
- Share food
- Pray together creatively
- Be together across the generations

It helps to keep to a recognizable format; everyone knows what to expect and so will feel more comfortable in participating:
- Have helpful attitudes
- Be reassuring
- Hold no prejudices over commitment
- Recognize the many demands already on those involved
- Normalization—sometimes life is rough and it's good to have people recognize that
- Recognize this is a journey for all
- Offer a sense of belonging
- Consider whether a safe place to feel vulnerable may be needed

If you are short of ideas for these belonging events, the *Creative Ways of Being Church* program gives a few examples:
- Karaoke night
- Memory Book
- Book Club
- Movie Night
- International Food Night
- Parish Weekend
- Parish Tour—has everyone seen all the parts of your parish?

- Garden Group
- Walkathon for a local charity
- A social event following Mass

Evangelization and catechesis are about inviting people to be active disciples of Christ—the vehicle to find and sustain faith—so always claim the event for Christ in prayer, and invite people to get involved in some form of learning and/or pastoral ministry. Never be afraid of asking people to help tidy up. There are few greater messages about belonging in a community than being given a job to do.

These ideas will be expanded in further chapters as a key way of building up an effective community of disciples in the body of Christ.

FIFTEEN

Evangelizing those who have not heard the Word of God

As the parish becomes stronger as a community of disciples, we naturally reach a point where we want to share what we have with others. Today, so many people have not heard the Word of God, and it can be quite difficult to know where to start to evangelize, especially if a parish has not had much experience. To start, it makes sense to target a particular sector of the community. Then, with some experience, it becomes easier to target the next group.

The Catholic Church has a unique opportunity for reaching and evangelizing young parents through their parish schools. It makes lot of sense to target this group because they are the people who have the greatest influence on the faith of the next generation.

Over thirty million children in the world are in Catholic elementary schools (Agenzia Fides, 2010), most of which are connected to a parish. In the Western world, many parents of these children are apathetic toward the Church. The word "spiritual" seems to resonate positively with them, but "religion" does not.

Despite this, many parents still want their children to know Christ and have some understanding of faith, and so they send them to Catholic schools, even if they don't take them to Mass. Of course there are others who send their children to Catholic schools simply because the schools are perceived to have high standards and good values.

In countries such as United Kingdom and Canada where many Catholic schools are dependent upon public funding, it is not easy to suggest that a key function of a faith school is the evangelization of children, let alone their parents. A secular society is tolerant of religion, particularly if it is practiced in private, but the word "evangelization" tends to be associated with heavy-handed proselytizing, and evangelization is frequently discouraged, if not banned, from many state-funded faith schools. There is a real concern that this constant, not-so-subtle pressure against evangelization is slowly eroding faith formation into the subject of religious education—just another subject on the curriculum with no more value than history or geography.

However, family values built on a strong foundation of love are less likely to be seen as anything but beneficial, not just to the school, but also to the wider community and indeed to society itself. To speak of Christian love and Christian spirituality, as opposed to Christian religion, is not a misrepresentation. Love is what our faith is about, and it is exactly what our focus should be. A key element of successful evangelization and catechesis is to fully accept that faith is a journey. It takes a lifetime and more of practice to become love, because love is not just an intellectual choice.

If this is to happen within a school, it is important that it be initiated and coordinated by members of the parish, because all family groups in the parish—school- or parish-based—should always have their spiritual home in the parish community.

Rather than attempting to reach all parents in the school at the outset, this initiative can start with a meeting of new parents at the time that they enroll their children. The parish facilitators would seek to understand why the parents have chosen the school for their children. Parents should then be reminded that a school can only support what happens in the home and cannot be substitute for the family in instilling faith, love, and values.

> This role [of parents] in education is so important that only with difficulty can it be supplied where it is lacking. Parents are the ones who must create a family atmosphere animated by love and respect for God and man, in which the well-rounded personal and social education of children is fostered.   *GRAVISSIMUM EDUCATIONIS* 3

Parents would then be invited to form family groups to be family to each other by consciously and actively keeping Christ's commandment to love one another as he loves us. Explain how a family group operates. Initially, the family group leaders would be experienced members of the parish until the family group is well established.

To ensure that connectedness with their Eucharistic community, family groups should always be gently invited to:
- Participate in all the social activities of the parish.
- Attend special celebrations and feast days in the parish.
- Share their gifts and talents in the parish by joining small ministry groups.
- Attend school Masses in the parish.
- Attend RCIA programs if and when they feel called.
- Attend plenary sessions with all the other family groups in the parish.

As they get to know and participate in the richness and spirituality of an active community of disciples, we can be confident that through the gift of the Holy Spirit their journey into full communion with the Family of God in the body of Christ will continue and be sustained.

There needs to be a good working relationship based on trust and mutual respect between the parish and the school. Those parishioners involved should clearly understand that the primary role of the school is to educate children, and they should ensure that use of any school facilities should never interrupt lessons or undermine or place unreasonable demands on the teachers or management of the school.

■ Other opportunities for evangelization

It is not enough to put a great big welcome sign up outside the church and expect that people will flock to join on your terms. Like Jesus, we have to get out into the marketplace, the highways and the byways, to meet people where they are.

People are actively searching for spirituality without knowing that it can only be found in a relationship of communion with God and one another. In a politically correct society we are expected to behave as if "my faith is between God and me," and so in effect it has nothing to do with anyone around us. It is not spoken about, and the love of God is not shared. As a result, seekers are unlikely to experience the spirituality of a relationship with God and the community. We can only truly find God through each other in communion. The image and likeness of God is a loving, creative relationship. We are intended to be spiritual beings.

Because a church may be a "bridge too far" for many in the secular society, parishes need to set up satellite points of contact to meet people where they are. Here are a few examples to stimulate ideas:

- Ask a coffee shop in the town center to stay open one evening a week, and advertise it as a meeting place for people to come and talk to someone who is a good listener. If you can have a nun or a monk dressed in their habit, so much the better. People have great respect for people who have obviously made a serious commitment.

- Ask the local gym for space for people to join a session in meditation. Invite people to care for their spiritual well-being as well as their physical well-being. The gym is likely to be very receptive to anything that will increase foot traffic.

- Consider asking a local pub to make space available for Theology on Tap twice a month. These gatherings of a priest and young people in their twenties and thirties are proving very popular venues for talking about God in a relaxed, nonjudgmental setting.

- Have a coffee morning each week for young mothers. Always make sure that blessings and prayers are included at the beginning and end. Have a session on theological reflection, using Scripture, relating to the events in their lives.

- Start a Do It Yourself ministry for people to help with repairs and decorations in homes around the neighborhood. They can charge those who can afford it and use the funds raised to buy materials for those who can't afford to pay. Make sure there is always some social time for the group, and include prayer, blessings, and sessions for theological reflection, using Scripture, on the work they do.

Not every idea will work in every parish. There is nothing wrong in trying something and discovering that it does not work. This is quite normal and part of the work of building a community of disciples. All it means is that we need to keep listening for and understanding actual needs, continue to be innovative, and keep trying. It is not uncommon for something to be a resounding success in one part of town and not get off the ground in another.

■ Link to the parish

No matter whether it is the school or any other satellite of the parish, the objective is always to have every person find their place in the faith community of the parish. The people engaged in the schools and satellites will always be invited to parish socials and other events where they can get to know the Eucharistic community of the parish. They will always be made aware of and invited to attend the Masses in the parish that are focused toward children. If there is a parish retreat, they will be invited. When the RCIA course starts each year in the parish, they should be made aware of it, without any pressure. All these invitations to participate in parish life should be relaxed, welcoming, and gentle. Heavy-handed proselytizing does not work. We cannot dictate when the Holy Spirit will call them and give them the gift of faith.

■ Evangelizing those on "leave of absence"

Technically these people have heard the Word of God, but it may have been a long time ago, and their understanding of our relationship with God may have been interpreted in a different era. It is also quite possible that they may have had a negative experience and entering a church could hold no attraction. Most families know someone, perhaps a member of their own family, who has become disillusioned with the Church for whatever reason.

Inviting these people into active discipleship in family groups or small ministry could provide the practical and meaningful approach to living their faith that was missing and caused them to leave in the first place. If we are aware of a practical need somewhere in the parish, we could start by inviting them to help. If they enjoy the experience, and a Small Ministry Group exists for people with similar gifts and talents, they may be interested in joining that group. Make sure they are invited to parish social events.

It is quite possible that some of these people started questioning the practice of their faith in the Church and found many contradictions and hypocrisy that they could not reconcile. We need to engage with them to help move them forward to that inclusive universal Church I spoke of in Chapter Two.

SIXTEEN

The leadership challenge

Change only happens with effective leadership, but all too often people think that leadership means exercising the authority of office. Jesus instructed that this was not to happen in his Church:

> "You know that the rulers of the Gentiles lord it over them, and the great ones make their authority over them felt. But it shall not be so among you. Rather, whoever wishes to be great among you shall be your servant; whoever wishes to be first among you shall be your slave. Just so, the Son of Man did not come to be served but to serve and to give his life as a ransom for many."
>
> MATTHEW 20:25-28

Leadership is about inspiring others to change. Every Christian is called to lead others to Christ. To lead always implies a change of some sort; we don't lead others by standing still and remaining where we are. People who are in charge like to call themselves leaders, but if they don't inspire people to change, they are managers, and if they bring about change through fear, they are dictators, not leaders. John Quincy Adams knew what he was talking about when he spoke of leadership:

> "If your actions inspire others to dream more, learn more, do more and become more, you are a leader."

If dreams reflect our ability to hope, by this measure it is easily argued that Jesus is the greatest leader of all time. He has inspired more people than any other leader in history to hope more, learn more, do more, and become more. And yet on earth, he was in charge of nothing that was materially significant; he had no armies, and no official authority, or power of office. Lack of money did not prevent him from passing on the love of God, because love and pastoral care are about giving oneself. He did not need fear to get people to change. His method for this great leadership is a clear message that people can believe in; it is an invitation to a holy communion of love, involving acceptance, trust, consistency, transparency, knowledge, respect, and truth.

Too often we rely on our structures of power for leadership authority. It has been claimed that the organizational structure of the institutional church is the structured community that Christ created (cf. Dulles, *Models of the Church*), but there is little evidence to support this.

> Although it is difficult to assert that Jesus established anything like an institutional church, it is undeniable that that he called forth a community of disciples in order to share in and continue his mission to proclaim and realize the coming reign of God.   GAILLARDETZ, 2008, P. 32

This claim, however, promotes a style of leadership that leads to institutionalism. The structure instituted by Jesus was a

Community of Disciples, not the institutionalism that has been considered by some to be a valid model of Church.

> By institutionalism we mean a system in which the institutional element is treated as primary. From the point of view of this author, institutionalism is a deformation of the true nature of the Church—a deformation that has unfortunately affected the Church at certain periods of its history, and one that remains in every age a real danger to the institutional Church. A Christian believer may energetically oppose institutionalism and still be very much committed to the Church as an institution.
>
> DULLES, *MODELS OF THE CHURCH, EXPANDED EDITION,* P. 27

Every structure needs to be institutionalized if it is to survive across the generations, but "the structures of the Church must be seen as subordinate to its communal life and mission" (Dulles, *Models of the Church, Expanded Edition*, 2002, p. 185). The institutional governance, rituals, symbols, laws, and processes are there only to aid and support the members of the Church to live a life in Christ.

If a Community of Disciples is the model Christ established for a Church of love, what would a church of fear look like? Fear, of course, is the opposite of love. We seek to have power over others because of our fear of others having power over us. At one level, fear causes a reliance on the authority of office and distrust of the laity, which can breed resentment and disaffection, when people are discouraged from questioning, and prevented from using their gifts and talents to pass on God's love. At another level, fear causes the struggle for power we see today between the liberals and traditionalists, trading insults on blogs and threatening disruption, which prevents any meaningful dialogue to reach understanding.

Above all else, Church is the one place where it should be obvious, by our behavior, that there is only one truth from which all other truth flows:

God is love.

This is why God made us, just to love us.

This is why it is not possible to love without God being present.

This is why peace, joy, happiness, contentment, and wholeness can only be found in a Holy Communion with God and his creation.

This is why we have a free will to choose.

This is why, when we insisted on making bad choices, God took the only action that Love could take:

> For God so loved the world that he gave his only Son, so that everyone who believes in him might not perish but might have eternal life. For God did not send his Son into the world to condemn the world, but that the world might be saved through him. Whoever believes in him will not be condemned, but whoever does not believe has already been condemned, because he has not believed in the name of the only Son of God. And this is the verdict, that the light came into the world, but people preferred darkness to light, because their works were evil. For everyone who does wicked things hates the light and does not come toward the light, so that his works might not be exposed. But whoever lives the truth comes to the light, so that his works may be clearly seen as done in God.
>
> JOHN 3:16-21

That "God is love" is the truth to which all law and doctrine and dogma are subject. The truth is self-evident because when we love unconditionally, we experience the peace, the joy, and the contentment that we crave, which come from being with and knowing God. This is the truth that best informs our conscience, when we ask: "Is this the best way to choose the love that leads me and those around me into a Holy Communion with God?" It is this truth that we should always seek when we find the laws difficult to understand, because "Love does no evil to the neighbor; hence, love is the fulfillment of the law" (Rom 13:10).

If a Community of Disciples and a fear-filled struggle for power are at either end of a continuum, then you will find the faithful will be spread along its length, as we all struggle between self-serving power and self-giving love. However, by acknowledging this, we should be careful that we are not tempted to accept that this is just part of the human condition, and therefore something we can't do anything about. Leaders know that people tend to live up to what is expected of them, and if we have low expectations, little will change.

Christ has a different expectation. He reminds us that humankind was born in a state of original grace, and we are called to live in the image and likeness of God, for which we were created. In that expectation of us, Jesus did not compromise.

> Jesus said to him, "If you wish to be perfect, go, sell what you have and give to [the] poor, and you will have treasure in heaven. Then come, follow me." When the young man heard this statement, he went away sad, for he had many possessions. MATTHEW 19:21-22

Leaders are not afraid to set big goals, because they know that the ability to achieve them lies within what we believe. Henry Ford once said: "If you think you can or you think you can't, you're right!" I agree with that. John F. Kennedy had no idea how it was going to be done, but he created an expectation and a belief that the USA could achieve the seemingly impossible task of placing a man on the moon by the end of the decade, when he said:

> ...we choose to go to the moon in this decade and do the other things, not because they are easy, but because they are hard, because that goal will serve to organize and measure the best of our energies and skills, because that challenge is one that we are willing to accept, one we are unwilling to postpone, and one which we intend to win, and the others, too. *KENNEDY, 1961*

The irony is that the challenge Christ sets for us is not hard, unless we choose to make it so.

> Come to me, all you who labor and are burdened, and I will give you rest. Take my yoke upon you and learn from me, for I am meek and humble of heart; and you will find rest for your selves. For my yoke is easy, and my burden light. MATTHEW 11:28-30

God bends over backwards to help us realize Christ's expectation of us. We have the full resources of the Holy Spirit to draw on. But we struggle to trust God enough to give up our fear-driven measures of success and our self-reliance, in order to allow ourselves to believe truly and completely.

The reality of parish life in the Catholic Church is that no positive change is likely to happen unless it is *led* by the parish priest. Such is the authority of a priest that if he distrusts the laity and does not encourage or support them, little positive change will take place. Most Catholics (not all!) will avoid disagreement, let alone conflict, with a parish priest or the bishop. Instead, they just quietly empty the pews.

The last thing leadership means is that you should do it all yourself. Rather, it means that you encourage, enable, and support people to love and believe in themselves so that they want to do things for others and encourage them to pass that on. We are called to be leaders of leaders, building one another up to hope more, learn more, do more, and become more, just as Jesus did. This is what it means to love one another as Christ loves us. Remember that the vast majority of problems will not be caused by a person's attitude, but by a lack of knowledge and skill. Knowledge and skill problems are overcome through catechesis, teaching, and practice. Distrust, a problem of attitude, will always be a serious barrier to communion, because it gets in the way of people becoming what Christ is calling them to be.

Church is about people being involved in all five key purposes of discipleship, and leaders should encourage and inspire them to do this. Father Patrick Brennan is the former parish priest of Holy Family Parish in Chicago, Illinois. Over a period of twenty-three years, over half of that time in which he was pastor, the parish grew from zero to four thousand families. As of 2010, they had one hundred and forty ministry groups, and lifelong formation is considered to be a charism. They have one parish priest and around thirty employed staff. This is Fr. Pat's view of the co-responsibility of the laity:

> Vatican II reminded the church that ordained priests share in the ministry or priesthood of their local ordinary or bishop. In turn it has been my experience in all the parishes I have served in, but most of all in this parish that I have pastored, that parishioners share in my priesthood,

and all of us, connected with the archbishop of Chicago,
are really continuing the mission, the work, the priest-
hood, if you will, of Jesus Christ.   BRENNAN, 2007, P. 132

The point is that, irrespective of the size of the parish, co-responsible laity leads to growth and greater effectiveness in proclaiming the gospel. Leadership is most effective when we build
others up to become leaders of leaders and teachers of teachers.
Our most revered leaders are those who believe in us before we
do and so inspire us to become what we are capable of.

SEVENTEEN

Holy order in the parish

Any group of people needs some form of organization in order to function efficiently. What model of organization is best for a parish? A true business model isn't quite right—the typical parish is not motivated by profit and creation of wealth. However, like a business, a parish needs policies and procedures and organizational structures to maintain good order and ensure everyone is working hard to achieve the goals.

A parish is different in that it is motivated by relationships rather than by profit. First and foremost, we strive for a relationship with Christ, and because he is in each of us, we find him in each other. In an effective parish, members will have strong relationships with each other.

We have spoken before of the idea that a functional family is a good model for a parish, as this conjures up the right images of loving relationships. In reality, however, this is an incomplete model—everyone has their own idea, based on their own experience of a functional family, of how a family should operate. So, using the functional family as an organizational model is just too subjective. A more realistic organizational model for a parish would be an orchestra striving to play the most beautiful symphony of all: *God's Kingdom of Love.*

An orchestra exists for the listening pleasure of others. And as William Temple said, "The Church is the only society that exists for the benefit of those who are not its members." Members of an orchestra don't sit in the audience to observe and listen. They are active participants. Members of a parish should actively participate in Christ's mission of love to bring about the kingdom.

The conductor, the leader of the orchestra, interprets the symphony and ensures that everyone plays their part fully and appropriately. Too many of us are only too ready to outsource our obligations to the pastor, and all too often, some pastors prevent us from fully playing our part. The conductor does not play a note and cannot produce the symphony alone. Instead, the leader of the orchestra interprets the music and ensures that all the members are using their talents to the full, together producing the most wonderful symphony.

Many great orchestras don't have a resident conductor. Guest conductors come in from time to time for major concerts. The loss of a resident parish priest does not have to mean the end of a parish. A friend of mine in Ecuador has seventy-five village communities spread over a huge area in his parish. Each community continues to function effectively under lay leadership on a day-to-day basis even though they have Mass only once every three or four months.

During the apartheid regime in South Africa, Catholic missionary priests from Europe and elsewhere were viewed as subversive by the government who stopped letting them in to the country. So, South Africa experienced their priest shortage twenty to thirty years ago. Where members of the laity were enabled and prepared to step up to the plate, instead of closing churches, the communities thrived, and today vocations are on the increase in those parishes.

An orchestra plays the same symphony together, even if they are not all playing at the same time. As the body of Christ, we each have a different role to play, but if we try to play it alone, for our own benefit, it will create discord and a cacophony of noise that will drive people away.

The needs of the parish are greater than any individual, and no person should be allowed to prevent any other from using their gifts to the full or to undermine the parish mission. A symphony is about timing, harmony, and teamwork. A note that is willfully and consistently played out of tune or at the wrong time will destroy the efforts of the whole orchestra. No matter how technically skilled an individual is, the music of the symphony of the kingdom is love which builds people up, and no individual, not even the conductor, should be allowed to hold the orchestra for ransom.

There are different sections in an orchestra. Family Groups of families and Small Ministry Groups bring together people with similar objectives and gifts to meet those objectives. While each section plays its part, they remain a part of the whole. Small groups are not free to become exclusive cliques. Nor should a dominant personality within a group be allowed to lead that group off in a different direction. Parish leaders need to ensure that the practices within each group always conform to the parish mission and each group remains transparent and welcoming to all.

Each section, like each small group in a parish, has a role to play. The boundaries between each section are clear and understood by all. In a parish boundaries need to be equally clear to avoid confusion and to ensure that we each play our own part well in the body of Christ. No group is more important than another.

The little finger on a hand may not be an eye, but the body is incomplete and does not function as well without either.

An orchestra has expectations of its members. If people showed up when they felt like it and never practiced, its reputation would precede it and few would pay to attend a concert. In so many parishes nothing is expected of the laity, and they expect to be served the sacraments at their convenience. In the gospel, even the most inadequate—the woman at the well and the demoniac, for example—were expected to actively share the good news. Not just that; Jesus expected them to share it in the communities that rejected them. If we expect nothing, that's exactly what we will get.

An orchestra practices regularly. They don't stop learning when they leave school. They keep learning. They learn together, teaching each other to perform as a community in union—in communion. It is a lifetime journey to faith maturity. What we learned as a child is insufficient for the needs of a lifetime. We need to keep learning for ever better performances in the practice of our faith.

No doubt there are many other examples of orchestra behavior that reinforce that organizational model. Models are good to guide us, and if we have sufficient understanding of a model, it can provide a framework for us to think through and deal with day-to-day situations that arise.

A parish needs more than a model to maintain holy order. We are not just guided by common practices, but also by our values or principles. A parish will find common guiding principles very useful in dealing with those unpredictable issues that call for sound judgement in decision making and in managing the expectations of members.

■ Core guiding principles

Only a few principles or core values are necessary to guide a parish. The last thing you want is a rule book for every situation. It is also not good enough to assume that everyone knows and understands the purpose of a parish and what it stands for. The reality is that each person thinks that their view is the right one, and you'll find little consensus across the parish membership. (This situation can be intensified if the parish is a multicultural, multilingual community, where each culture brings its own values and traditions into the mix.)

The key purpose of the Church and therefore a parish is to help its members learn to love unconditionally. Let's quickly remind ourselves of the reasons for this:

- God is love. Anything other than love is not compatible with God. If we want to be one with God, then the whole purpose of our life is to learn how to become love so that we are compatible with him and can become one with him.
- The Two Great Commandments that Jesus taught us make it clear that everything else depends on us loving God, our neighbor, and ourselves.
- When we love unconditionally, we turn from sin, because sin is a refusal to love.

If, as a parish we accept that learning to love unconditionally is a core value or principle to guide us, then we can use this principle to guide us whenever we are faced with choices in what we do or how we do it. When we are faced with different options, we have one or two questions to ask. Which will promote unconditional love more:

- taking the time to explain what the issue is and asking for help in resolving it, or simply making a change and expecting people to adapt?
- insisting on taking instructions only from an already overworked priest, or working with anyone who is genuinely trying their best for the good of the parish?
- trusting people to be guided by this key principle and encouraging them to get involved, or not allowing them to do anything for fear the result may not be perfect?
- waiting for the few who never arrive on time and keep everyone else waiting, or respect the effort people have made to volunteer their time by starting and finishing at the stated times?

I'm sure you get the idea about how key principles are used to guide us.

Another key principle might be that the parish is *mission-driven*. In other words, we actively accept our call to participate in God's work of reconciling the whole of creation to himself. The parish will focus its efforts on helping to bring about God's kingdom in this world. Again this principle, which calls members to look at the world beyond the parish's borders and to see their place in the wider picture, will help to guide the parish in creating holy order in its efforts and behavior.

Another effective core guiding principle should be for everyone—priests, religious, and laity—to accept co-responsibility for the apostolate: the life and mission of the Church.

And of course, a key principle must be that the parish will strive to achieve the greater good for the whole parish in any conflict of priorities.

I am not suggesting that these could not be better stated or that the list is complete. However, I caution again against having too many guiding principles as they will lose their collective purpose and lead to nit-picking arguments. This is about getting people to concentrate on the intention and develop the right collective attitude for effectiveness. It's not about policies and procedures.

Having said that, for the sake of efficiency it is useful to make it clear what is expected of people, especially to ensure that groups of people working together have a common purpose and objectives that everyone understands.

▣ Clear roles and responsibilities

In mentioning roles and responsibilities, there is a distinct possibility that some people will be saying: "You just said a parish is not a business. It is ridiculous to expect us to have things like defined roles and responsibilities and organizational structures." As I mentioned earlier, the members of an orchestra have clear roles, and their responsibilities in producing the symphony are very specific for everyone to know. They may not call them roles and responsibilities, but they are written down on the sheets of music, and everyone depends on them to function together effectively.

If this feels too business-like, perhaps it will come as a surprise for some to know that the business hierarchical structure that we know and understand so well is less than 100 years old. It was copied from the Catholic Church and the Army in the 1920s as an effective way of organizing and managing large numbers of people working together. As one of the oldest and most successful institutions on the planet, the Catholic Church has had to find and develop ways to organize itself to keep the faith pure, ensure effective communication, and proclaim the gospel globally. The

Catholic Church was the first corporate body to practice global-
ization many centuries before business caught up. It's no wonder
that business has been able to learn so much from the Church to
achieve success.

Even the small group of apostles obviously had specific roles
and responsibilities. We know for example from a comment at the
Last Supper that Judas was the treasurer for the apostles because
he kept their money bag: "Some thought that since Judas kept the
money bag, Jesus had told him, 'Buy what we need for the feast,'
or to give something to the poor" (Jn 13:29).

Any group of people needs to organize itself if it is to sustain
itself and grow. The bigger the group gets, the more formal this
needs to be, in order to prevent people from duplicating and wast-
ing effort, ensuring the right people are doing the right things,
arranging for new needs to be met, and preventing mixed and
confused messages being transmitted.

This is not about pigeon-holing people or being unnecessar-
ily bureaucratic. It is about having enough structure in place to
ensure effective communication so as to avoid confusion. An excellent example of how organizational problems were dealt with
in the early Church by clarifying roles and responsibilities is given
in Acts 6:

> At that time, as the number of disciples continued to
> grow, the Hellenists complained against the Hebrews
> because their widows were being neglected in the daily
> distribution. So the Twelve called together the com-
> munity of the disciples and said, "It is not right for us
> to neglect the word of God to serve at table. Brothers,
> select from among you seven reputable men, filled with
> the Spirit and wisdom, whom we shall appoint to this
> task, whereas we shall devote ourselves to prayer and to

the ministry of the word." The proposal was acceptable to the whole community, so they chose Stephen, a man filled with faith and the holy Spirit, also Philip, Prochorus, Nicanor, Timon, Parmenas, and Nicholas of Antioch, a convert to Judaism. They presented these men to the apostles who prayed and laid hands on them. ACTS 6:1-6

It is not uncommon for some parishioners to refuse the leadership of anyone but the priest. A sure way to ensure the decline of the Church is for the laity to refuse to work with each other in a parish.

By the same token, we have also seen some people who quickly assume a greater authority than they have been delegated and start bossing all and sundry around in the parish. This approach also undermines the efforts of parishioners as they become demotivated by the lack of respect shown to them and withdraw.

While it may take some effort initially, having well-documented roles and responsibilities for each small ministry group will reduce stress, clarify what is expected of people, avoid time being wasted, and prevent potential conflict. In the long run the small amount of initial effort will be repaid many times over in facilitating a more effective, happier, and faster-growing community.

Defining the roles and responsibilities of a Small Ministry Group does not have to be complex, particularly as generic instructions that apply to all Small Ministry Groups can be recorded once in a parish manual. The information required for clarity of the role and responsibilities is shown on the next page.

See the Appendix for a comprehensive guide to effective discipleship training for Small Ministry Groups.

SMALL MINISTRY GROUP

ROLE AND RESPONSIBILITIES

Date: _____

Name of Parish: _____
_____

Name of Small Ministry Group: _____
_____

Ministry of the Group: _____
_____

Responsible to: _____
_____

Coordinates with: _____
_____

Based at: _____
_____

Key responsibilities and accountabilities: _____
_____

Things for which the Small Ministry Group is not
responsible: _____
_____
_____

■ Conflict resolution

Last but by no means least, holy order demands that conflicts in a parish are not just managed but are actually resolved. Even in the best of orchestras there will be conflict. A parish has huge potential for conflict because for most of us, our faith is at the core of our values. We come from different backgrounds and have different life experiences. We have different experiences of Christ and so we have different values. We also have different personality types. As a result, we are never going to totally agree with one another, and we will frequently rub each other up the wrong way.

One of the things I have learned about conflict is that "Least said, soonest mended" is just not true. Hurt and anger can be sustained and nurtured under a veneer of politeness for generations.

Why are we so afraid of dealing with conflict? After all, what is conflict but a difference of opinion? The Good Lord loves diversity. We are not expected to all have the same opinion, and we are all entitled to have an opinion. Instead of breaking down relationships, conflicts can be opportunities to get to know one another better and build stronger relationships. We don't have to agree on everything to work with one another. We just need to find common ground and respect our differences in opinion. We can easily agree to disagree on some issues.

It is not the purpose of this book to teach conflict resolution skills. Others have already done so far more effectively than I could. The point is, those skills are easily learned, and a Community of Disciples should make it a habit to practice those skills to build up the Church. If you are looking for a good resource, I recommend the book *The Eight Essential Steps to Conflict Resolution* by Dudley Weeks, Ph.D. It reads easily and is very practical.

I find I need to keep reminding myself that forgiving someone is more beneficial for me than it will ever be for the person I forgive. Forgiveness takes back the power they have over me that makes me want to seek revenge and feel anxious, stressed, demotivated, depressed, and sorry for myself. When I forgive, even if the other party has not repented, I take back control of my life, and I become free to love again.

EIGHTEEN

Having realistic expectations

Naturally we all want the Sure Thing—the quick, simple answer that is easy to implement, costs nothing, and can happen overnight. If nothing else is clear about becoming a community of disciples, finding a quick-fix solution isn't in the cards. Church is a way of life—a journey. No book can ever be a clearly marked, sign-posted roadmap to the kingdom.

Always be realistic. Not everyone is going to come on board at the first invitation. There are different kinds of people: *pioneers*—people who make things happen; *naysayers*—people who try to prevent things happening; *observers*—people who watch things happen; *preoccupied*—people who wonder what happened.

Identify, encourage, and support the pioneers. Keep engaged with the naysayers. They are often people who have had their fingers burned in the past, and they may have valuable lessons to share. Naturally cautious, once they come on board and believe, they become the champions of the effort. If they are ignored, they will often split the parish and leave or continually throw stones from the sidelines. Keep exhorting the observers to come on board and discover what they are missing. Hands-on experience can make them very enthusiastic. Find ways to keep communicating with the preoccupied, and try to convert them into observers, if not participants. They are often in the majority and when they suddenly wake up and don't like what they see, they can rapidly become naysayers or leave.

Jesus did not promise us that convincing others would be easy.

> And he spoke to them at length in parables, saying: "A sower went out to sow. And as he sowed, some seed fell on the path, and birds came and ate it up. Some fell on rocky ground, where it had little soil. It sprang up at once because the soil was not deep, and when the sun rose it was scorched, and it withered for lack of roots. Some seed fell among thorns, and the thorns grew up and choked it. But some seed fell on rich soil, and produced fruit, a hundred or sixty or thirtyfold. Whoever has ears ought to hear."
>
> MATTHEW 13:3-9

When I find myself trying too hard to rely on my own efforts, the Holy Spirit gives me a prod to remind me that my job is to keep on faithfully planting seeds and to leave him to worry about the things I have no control over.

Expect people to claim that whatever you are proposing may work elsewhere but it won't work in your parish: "Maybe this works in Africa or the UK, but this is the US. It won't work here. We are different." Another excuse I hear is: "This may work for the middle classes but my parish is full of working-class people. It won't work here. We are different." I have yet to visit a nation or a corporation or a government department that will not use a variation of the excuse that "We are different" to avoid change. Nobody has yet explained to me what works for them instead. Nobody claims that their purpose is not to learn to love so they too can become one with God. Nobody denies that love means getting out and serving others. Nobody denies that we find our humanity through each other and we can only be Christian in community. Sadly, just the excuse for inaction is offered—"We are different."

The point here is that if you embark on the journey to become a community of disciples, you should expect people to resist. The members of your parish are not going to be taking your arm off to form small ministry groups. For many, this is not what they expect Church to be. Worse still, the fact that change is necessary will be seen by some as an indictment of all the hard work they have done for decades for the Church. They will be in denial, claiming there is no need to improve.

Jesus knew what he was talking about. He knew that a change to a life in Christ was not going to be without conflict, and he also knew that those who would oppose it most would be the people closest to us:

> "Do not think that I have come to bring peace upon the earth. I have come to bring not peace but the sword. For I have come to set a man 'against his father, a daughter against her mother, and a daughter-in-law against her mother-in-law; and one's enemies will be those of his household.' Whoever loves father or mother more than me is not worthy of me, and whoever loves son or daughter more than me is not worthy of me; and whoever does not take up his cross and follow after me is not worthy of me." MATTHEW 10:34-38

No matter where you are in the world, a life in Christ is countercultural. It is different. That's the whole point.

◼ Remaining in control

Humans have a great need to be in control, which is why they need certainty about things upon which their values are based. Your biggest "enemies" in this change will be in your own parish, and members of the parish will have "enemies" in their own households, because you may be shaking the foundation upon which people have built their values, their understanding of Church, and what it means in their lives. People cope and are better able to remain in control when they know what to expect.

◼ Resolve

Jesus was clearly determined that change would happen even at the expense of family conflict and dissent. If we are following Jesus' direction, then we see the resolve we should have. Change is not for the fainthearted. There are no guarantees of success, but the death of a parish community is assured if nothing changes. If you accept that doing nothing is not an option, then the next step and each step afterwards have to be taken with firm resolve. There has to be an acceptance that there is no turning back. It is the same acceptance that Jesus had, that his way was going to bring conflict and disrupt otherwise good relationships, even in close families. He did not turn back when things became tough.

◼ Listen

Fortunately, a lot can be done to minimize the negative impact of change, but it takes time and effort. While Jesus was prepared to accept the consequences of his resolve, we know that his nature was not to hurt people, if there was any other way. As we embark in bringing about a community of active disciples in the parish, even as we remain true to our resolve, we need to try to take as many people along with us as possible, and do so in a way that does not cause unnecessary distress.

It's quite normal for any group to claim this new approach will not work with them. Remember always that silence does not mean acceptance. It could just as easily mean a serious case of passive aggression. Continually engage with people and seek their opinions. Make a real effort to listen and understand what they are really saying. Just because someone does not like the way you are doing things does not mean that they may not have a better way of doing it. Wherever possible allow people to do things their way as long as the desired result is achieved. This will ensure that people taken ownership and do a good job.

Ask what might work. If you get an answer, that can often be your starting point. Start where folks are at and build from there. This approach to being a community of disciples does not negate any of the good work that is already being done in parishes. It provides a structure that enables that work to be more effective. Be ready to take things one step at a time.

■ Avoid surprises

Avoid surprising people. People hate surprises. It upsets their sense of being in control.

One priest I know decided that he was going to move the pews in their church so that they faced each other from either side of the church. The altar would be on one side of the congregation while the lectern would be at the other. He did this without warning, and the surprised reaction he got when people arrived for Mass on Sunday was not the one he was hoping for. To put it mildly, there was an uproar. "I don't come to Mass to look at her!"

was one comment. The pews were returned to their original positions, and he is now firmly of the opinion that it is not possible to make changes like that in his parish.

A change of that type needs to be preceded by appropriate catechesis, explaining the need for communion and participation of all at Mass and clarifying how making such a change could symbolically enhance the meaning and the purpose of Mass. There should be an opportunity for discussion and for concerns to be raised. Everyone should be asked to come along and share in the work of moving things about, and perhaps a special Mass celebrated to pray that love will overcome any animosity we might feel, and that the changes will help to bring us closer to one another in communion.

■ Sponsorship

Change does not happen without a sponsor. Who is the sponsor? The sponsor is the person who has the greatest power and influence to make it happen. Everyone will look to that person to legitimize the change. In the diocesan Church, the key sponsor is the bishop. If the bishop is totally behind the change, priests will have the courage to step up to the plate and accept their responsibility as the key sponsor in the parish. The point here is that unless the priest is seen to be totally committed to the change, the hearts and minds of the parishioners will not change and nothing will happen. Such is the power that priests have to influence their flock.

It is not enough to give approval. People need to know that the leader believes in it and is determined to make it happen. Unless they perceive this commitment to the cause, everyone will give verbal affirmation to the importance of the change and do nothing. The pastor needs to talk about the change at every meeting and mention it in a relevant way in every homily. He needs to give progress reports. When things go wrong, as they inevitably will, he needs to remind everyone that taking a wrong turn on a journey does not mean failure—unless you give up and turn back. Rather, taking a wrong turn is merely a lesson learned about something that does not work in a particular situation.

This sounds like a lot of work, and no sponsor ever has the time to be totally involved in the change project. The wise priest will delegate responsibility and get regular updates on progress from those he has entrusted with responsibility. The sponsor does not do all the work; he enables it to happen and exhorts others to do it.

■ Change is personal

Change happens one person at a time. This is hard work until there is a critical mass of adherents to the new way, and then most of the rest will follow. Most people are not naturally altruistic. For people to change, they need to know the answer to the question: "What's in it for me?" But just because someone can see the benefits for themselves does not mean that they will be prepared to be a pioneer.

People need to know that others will support the change and that they are not going to be left exposed if it does not work, even if they perceive it to be a good idea.

All this is nothing new:

> It must be considered that there is nothing more difficult to carry out, nor more doubtful of success, nor more dangerous to handle, than to initiate a new order of things.
>
> For the reformer has enemies in all those who profit by the old order, and only lukewarm defenders in all

those who would profit by the new order, this lukewarm-
ness arising partly from fear of their adversaries,...and
partly from the incredulity of mankind, who do not truly
believe in anything new until they have had actual experience of it.

Thus it arises that on every opportunity for attacking
the reformer, his opponents do so with the zeal of parti-
sans, the others only defend him half-heartedly, so that
between them he runs great danger.

THE PRINCE—NICCOLO MACHIAVELLI (1532)

▓ Get people on board

It is a good idea first to take the time to persuade the natural leaders and influencers in the parish. These are the people who need
to be involved in developing the strategies and the plans to make
it happen. The more they invest in making it work, the more they
take ownership and convince others to join in.

▓ Communication

No matter how much you communicate, it will never be enough.
Effective change demands endless communication. It needs to be
consistent, and every available form of media, homily, and conversation should be used. The message should always relate relevance of the change to the current situation so that people come
to understand the change in a variety of contexts. People need to
know what a community of disciples means in the classroom, at
Mass, on the street, in the press, establishing liaisons with local
government, and in every other situation.

■ Track progress

Make sure you track progress. It is not enough to talk about something and let people interpret that to mean whatever they think it does. Have a clear vision of what a community of disciples looks like for you, and regularly evaluate the progress you are making toward bringing that vision to reality. When things are going off on a tangent, as they will, evaluations and reviews will help to keep everyone on track. This will focus and sustain the change.

■ When things go wrong

Expect things to go wrong and when they do, expect a great number of people to hold that apparent failure up as proof that the change is not a good idea. By implication, change means doing something you have not done before, and it involves a level of pioneering. Pioneers don't know the way. They *find* the way. Inevitably there will be mistakes. These are not failures—they are just signposts to what does not work in the way you tried it. Just because something worked in a parish down the road does not mean it will work in the same way in your parish without any adaptation. No two parishes are in the same place at the same time.

When things go wrong, first smile, then help to clean up the mess, learn the lesson, and start again, taking that lesson into consideration. Don't be distracted by the noise of the nay-sayers.

NINETEEN

Saints of the new millennium

L iving our faith is not just about structure, gifts, knowledge, and skill. We tend to place a huge emphasis on knowledge and skill and ignore attitude when we recruit and select people for jobs. Many years ago I heard of an analysis of the proportional contribution that *knowledge*, *skill*, and *attitude* each made in determining the success of an organization. This research disclosed that attitude contributed ninety-three percent of the success factor, while knowledge and skill together only contributed seven percent. Given a reasonable level of intelligence you can teach knowledge and skill to anyone who has the enthusiasm and drive to succeed. Attitude, however, is best influenced through consultation, respect, trust, and the leader's belief that the people involved can produce the desired result.

More than anything else, I would submit that it is not knowledge or skill, but an attitude of genuine acceptance and love that will inspire people to want to live a life in Christ as his disciple.

By its nature Christianity, or for that matter any religion, is idealistic. Often, when we fail to live up to those ideals, we are accused of being hypocrites. When we promote one ideal that contradicts another, we rapidly lose credibility. It is in the nature of the human condition to strive for the security of certainty, and when we find our certainty is built on sand and can easily crumble, we can quickly lose faith. We need to know that we are right, and sometimes that need can blind us to our true purpose.

But it is not enough to be right. We have to be effective. We do not have to give up our ideals to be effective, but we do have to be pragmatic about the way we strive to achieve them in the real world.

We cannot self-righteously blame those who do not blindly accept our views for their failure to hear the Word of God. If we want to welcome people into the Church, it is not enough to put up a welcome sign over the door and invite them in on our terms. Jesus went out into the marketplace and met people on their terms. This does not mean that he accepted their behavior, but he did accept their right to choose that behavior, while at the same time giving them another choice. He recognized that as creatures of God they were far more than their behavior, and he went far beyond simply spelling out the *law* to explain why people needed to change.

In practice many Christian denominations overemphasize moral theology at the expense of pastoral theology. Moral theology, in practice, tends to emphasize the passive "Thou shalt not…" commandments. It tends to focus on what we should not do, rather than encouraging us to explore the person we could be. When we overemphasize what we should not be doing, we leave people in a passive state of not actively committing sin. We encourage them to stop the sins of commission, but we still leave them with the sins of omission—a failure to act to become love. When we emphasize the sinfulness of the human condition, we also subconsciously create an expectation that invites people to sin because that's what sinners do. Subconsciously we react: "I am nothing but a poor sinner, so what else can anyone expect of me?"

Our energy is spent in pointing out sin and trying to drag people away from it while subconsciously confirming to them that that is where they belong.

Just to stop committing sin is to remain passive. How often have we heard: "I'm not a bad person. I haven't murdered anyone. I don't steal. I don't beat up my wife. I don't abuse children"?

Christianity is not passive. It's not about avoiding doing bad things. Christianity is about the action of striving to become love so that we can become one with God and one another. Love is the action of God in us as we care for and serve others.

When we concentrate on telling people what they should not be doing, we fail to encourage them to do what they should be doing. We fail to emphasize the greater importance of the active "Thou shalt…" commandments. Pastoral theology emphasizes the active "Thou shalt…" commandments, most particularly the Two Great Commandments: "You shall love the Lord, your God, with all your heart, with all your soul, and with all your mind… You shall love your neighbor as [you love] yourself" (Mt 22:37–38 [NJB]).

No doubt some will say that the first step to keeping the Great Commandments is to get people to stop the sins of commission. I think it would be far more effective to encourage people to do what they should be doing to accomplish their purpose on this planet: learning how to love. Sin is a refusal to love—an action that turns us from God, who is love. It follows then that action to become love makes sin impossible during that action. Pastoral theology is a call to action to become love. In support of this pastoral theology we need a moral theology that encourages us to think about the kind of person we could be.

We need to emphasize pastoral theology for the reasons Jesus gave us: so his joy may be in us, our joy may be complete, and we may be his friends:

As the Father loves me, so I also love you. Remain in my love. If you keep my commandments, you will remain in my love, just as I have kept my Father's commandments and remain in his love. I have told you this so that my joy may be in you and your joy may be complete. This is my commandment: love one another as I love you. No one has greater love than this, to lay down one's life for one's friends. You are my friends if you do what I command you.

JOHN 15:9-14

I chatted with a young woman in her very early twenties who is a street pastor. Some may wonder how anyone could possibly be joyful about staying up all night to help drunk and drugged people get home safely, especially when these people inflict it upon themselves and are often abusive instead of being appreciative. And yet this woman was bubbling over with enthusiasm and joy for the work she was doing. Every hour she goes out to serve others is an hour of her life that can never be replaced. She has laid down those hours of her life for her friends—the greatest love of all. Christ's joy, at working through her to be out there helping even those who deliberately place themselves in harm's way, week after week, was palpable in her. She radiated his love as she told me her story.

Father John Woolley truly was inspired in his book *I Am With You* when he wrote: "Where there is hope, where there is self-forgetfulness, where concern for others takes over from self, joy need not be longed for; it has become part of you!" (1984, p. 161).

When Christ's joy is in you because you are an active channel for expressing his love to others, sin is something foreign and abhorrent. You are one with God and your neighbor. You have become love.

Jesus did not ask people to repent before he healed, fed, and clothed them. They repented because they were welcomed by him, cared for, and loved. They did it because they experienced his love, not because they feared him or wanted to obey the law.

When we offer little else besides the Holy Eucharist for people to give expression to their faith, then, by default, they feel excluded in practice from the Church if they are not in communion. Their natural reaction is that the Church's role is to stand in judgment of them. We are then perceived as an exclusive church where only those who keep its laws are welcomed. And when we fail to live up to our own laws, as we do, we are considered to be hypocrites, applying one law for the privileged and another for the rest. When we are quick to judge others, they soon become quick to judge us. There is no point in us crying foul.

A couple married in a civil ceremony brought their child to a parish for instruction for first reconciliation. They were obviously enjoying being involved in the preparation, and so the parish priest asked if they would not like to be received into communion with the Church. When they asked what that would involve, he said they would have to first get married in the Church. "But we are married," they said. With little understanding of Church teaching, they perceived the invitation to be a criticism of them. No doubt in this day and age they felt they had demonstrated their responsibility and commitment by actually getting married. They were hurt and angry and dropped out of their involvement in the parent's group. "Well, that was that. Young people today are just not willing to accept the moral teachings of the Church," the priest told me in frustration.

We have no idea at what point on their pilgrimage through life the Holy Spirit will offer the gift of faith to someone. It is true that sometimes the Holy Spirit calls on us to extend that invitation on his behalf, but when we do, we need to be sensitive and not demand that people change their ways before they come to know Christ. In the example of the young couple, perhaps it would have been more effective to invite them to start exploring their faith together, to understand more about discipleship and a life in Christ. Conversion to a life in Christ is a journey, and Christian marriage is intended to aid and support that journey, rather than to be an end in itself or worse still, become a barrier to embarking on the journey. Once people start trying to live a life in Christ, marriage in the Church is likely to become something to be desired rather than being seen as an obligation. For the teachings of the Church to be effective, people need to understand why they exist in the first place. They are not necessarily self-evident in the values of a secular society.

In order to share the love of God and explain the teachings of the Church, we need to welcome and form relationships with people. As a result, they may become more willing to accept the invitation when the Holy Spirit chooses to give it. All relationships have their ups and downs. Especially when people are not in communion and cannot receive the Holy Eucharist, they should be encouraged to engage in the activities of the Church to experience and share the love of Christ through fellowship, learning, and service. As long as we keep inviting people to remain in relationship with the Church, the chance that they will be received or return to communion increases dramatically.

Saints are just sinners who keep trying to learn to love. It is much easier to keep trying when we are supported by our community and the people who love us. I'm sure we all know of families that have rejected a member because they don't conform to what is expected of them, and we know of the misery that follows for all concerned. They may have chosen the wrong career, married the wrong person, or perhaps they hang out with the wrong people instead of doing what we believe they should.

From the gospel it is highly likely that Jesus had this same experience with some of the members of his own family:

> He came to his native place and taught the people in their synagogue. They were astonished and said, "Where did this man get such wisdom and mighty deeds? Is he not the carpenter's son? Is not his mother named Mary and his brothers James, Joseph, Simon, and Judas? Are not his sisters all with us? Where did this man get all this?" And they took offense at him. But Jesus said to them, "A prophet is not without honor except in his native place and in his own house." And he did not work many mighty deeds there because of their lack of faith.
>
> MATTHEW 13:54-58

Why would Jesus be despised in his own place? Is it perhaps that he embarrassed them by mixing with sinners, prostitutes, and tax collectors? Of course, with hindsight, it is easily argued that he was busy converting these people. When he met with these people repeatedly, accepting them as God's creatures, eating and drinking with them, and even joking and laughing with them despite the fact that in all probability many never changed, could some members of his family have found that excuse a bit lame?

How often do we misunderstand the family that we know and love? How much easier is it to misunderstand and judge people in the community that we know little about? The fact is, so much still has to be revealed to us:

> "And when he comes he will convict the world in regard to sin and righteousness and condemnation: sin, be-

cause they do not believe in me; righteousness, because I am going to the Father and you will no longer see me; condemnation, because the ruler of this world has been condemned.

I have much more to tell you, but you cannot bear it now. But when he comes, the Spirit of truth, he will guide you to all truth. He will not speak on his own, but he will speak what he hears, and will declare to you the things that are coming. He will glorify me, because he will take from what is mine and declare it to you. Everything that the Father has is mine; for this reason I told you that he will take from what is mine and declare it to you."

JOHN 16:8-15

"I have much more to tell you, but you cannot bear it now." Are we yet ready for full revelation? Or has it perhaps already happened? After two thousand years, is there anything left to reveal? The Church teaches that there is much to learn. We do not yet love unconditionally. We certainly don't have all the answers.

I know that many people need the certainty of rules and regulations to guide us and also create a sense of understanding and control. Jesus did not come to change the law or throw it out. But he got really angry with people who set the law above God's invitation to love. There is no doubt that the Church would not have been able to grow and share the good news without laws and a strong institution to guide and sustain it across the generations. As an effective Church the laws have changed and will continue to change over the generations. We have an obligation to understand the reasons behind the law and be able to explain why it is important to follow each law, rather than blindly insist that people merely comply.

Jesus did not tell us to be monogamous and faithful in marriage because he wanted to lay down the law. He knows that a stable family unit grounded in love, where each member is more committed to the other members of the family than their own selfish desires or rights, is the most effective and common way to experience unconditional love—which is the way to God. Over the generations we have learned that people are most likely to adhere to that commitment and become unconditional love if everyone around them witnesses that commitment, also considers it to be important, and supports them in their efforts.

Sometimes the reasons for a law no longer exist, and then it becomes meaningless. When this happens, it may fall into disuse and in time may be formally eliminated from the code of the law. It is only when we continue to strive to understand the reasoning behind the law that the law can fulfill its purpose effectively—i.e., to lead us to become love, so we can become one with God. Always search for the love that the law is intended to lead us to, in order to understand the law. When the purpose of love is missing from a law, there is a real risk that it will lead people away from God.

A full understanding of the law is not a prerequisite for faith, or for sharing the good news. After all, if we all loved one another as Jesus loves us, we would have no need of laws. There can never be a cut-and-dried final and complete set of laws that will remain true for all time. For this reason, the Church teaches us that our conscience must be our ultimate guide. The Magisterium has a well-established record of amending the laws that guide us from generation to generation. Sometimes we think they may be a little slow, but the law is not something to be changed with each season's fashions.

As a Church we have a responsibility to consider the spirit and intention of the law and to use it to inform our conscience before making decisions. Ideally, the discernment of our conscience should try to always go beyond the question "Does this prevent me from being in a loving communion with God and my neighbor?" to "How would this help me better to be in a loving communion with God and my neighbor?" Remember that love is always a call to action.

While the law that guides us may change as society changes, there is one truth we can always feel secure in: God is love, and any effort on our part to become love and so help others to also become love, so we can all become one with God, is at the very foundation upon which the whole law and the prophets depend. Without that, Jesus tells us, the law effectively means nothing. Will we ever get perfect love right in our lifetime on earth? Not a chance. But as long as we keep getting up and trying again to become love, sainthood is guaranteed.

> Love does no evil to the neighbor; hence, love is the fulfillment of the law. ROMANS 13:10

TWENTY

Sustaining parish development

am proposing a Community of Disciples as a guide for ongoing parish development. This is not some program that will come to an end, because we are intended to be a holy community. It is simply a structured way of doing the work we were called to do.

Some may look at all that I have suggested and feel that their parish is not big enough to do all the things I suggest need to be done. This is just not true. Jesus did all that I am suggesting and more with just twelve apostles. I have taken this approach into small parishes, and they have started with just one Small Ministry Group focused on welcome.

When Pope Gregory the Great commissioned St. Augustine of Canterbury to evangelize the Anglo-Saxons, he told him: "Climbing the highest mountain starts with the first step." It does not matter that you don't have a clear roadmap for the journey, and the road ahead may seem dark and forbidding. All you need to see is the next step, and as you take each step, the direction of the step after that will become clearer. Yes, it is likely that you will make mistakes. You will be frustrated with the inevitable criticism from the naysayers pointing to the mistakes as proof that this effort was doomed to failure from the start. As I've noted before in this book, mistakes aren't failure; they are simply lessons on what does not work. Learn those lessons and keep going. It is human nature to always look up and see the mountain that still has to be climbed. Just as you reach what you thought was a peak, you discover that it is the top of a foothill, and a new and higher peak appears in front of you. This is the nature of the pilgrimage to the kingdom. You need to stop at regular intervals to take stock of progress by looking back to recognize what has been achieved and devise ways to build on those achievements. Otherwise, people will just see the mountain ahead, and energy will start sapping every time the naysayers open their mouths: "We started a welcome group a year ago. Aside from these few things that happened, not much has changed. We haven't become one big happy family. What's the point of starting more groups?"

The Church functions around the cycles of the liturgical year, and an effective community of disciples is no different. It will function best when its activities reflect the seasons of the liturgical calendar.

The Triduum, the Three Days of Easter, are at the core of the Christian faith, and the Three Days reflect our life in Christ.

Holy Thursday reflects our relationship in Holy Communion with God and each other. The Last Supper inspires us to strive for that close companionship and friendship with Jesus and each other. At the Last Supper he also invited us to accept and become his body to carry on the work he started. The agony in the Garden reminds us of how soon even those closest to Jesus can still fall asleep after receiving the Holy Eucharist and forget about his call to mission. Despite our inadequacies, he continues to rely on us. His faith in us inspires us to hope.

Good Friday reminds us of the absolute commitment of unconditional love—the sacrifice of our will to the will of God. Christ died for us, and he asks us to lay down our lives, minute by minute, in service to our neighbor. Just as he forgave his persecutors in their act of persecution, he calls on us to forgive even when there is no repentance. Only through unconditional forgiveness can we become love. In our darkest hours he places on us this seemingly impossible demand to become even more vulnerable and to risk people taking further advantage of us. This sacrifice is necessary so that we can release any anger, desire for revenge, self-righteousness, and fear that can hold us back from love. To accept this sacrifice calls for great faith and belief that, in spite of becoming vulnerable, it will be possible to set right what is wrong.

Easter Sunday. In the resurrection we realize that in accepting Christ's body at the Last Supper, we pass through the sacrifice of the cross to a share in the joy of the fruits of unconditional love. As we come to appreciate that only love can truly set right what is wrong, we experience Christ's joy in us, and our joy becomes complete, just as he promised, and we willingly become activists for Christ as his disciples—learners and workers to bring about the kingdom. We become the sacrament of the Holy Eucharist as we pass on God's gift of love to others.

The meaning and purpose of life, being fully human, living a life of real joy as God intended when he created us, is contained in those Three Days. Every Mass reflects this and is a renewed call to be fully human and fully engaged in God's mission for us to become love so we can be one with God and one another in Holy Communion.

It makes sense, then, that the celebration of the Triduum in a parish is highly likely to reflect the state of a parish's efforts to become a community of disciples. Because of this and its great meaning in our life in Christ, an evaluation of the Triduum each year will give a good overall opportunity to look back, see what has been achieved, and help to refocus the parish for the year ahead.

While the overall evidence of improvement in becoming a community of disciples will be reflected in the Three Days of Easter, the detailed evaluation would start with Lent, a natural time for reflection on the progress we are making on our journey to the kingdom. In this time of reflection it would also make sense to start planning for the year ahead. Existing Small Ministry Groups will put their plans for the next year together, and the parish leadership team will consider the overall pastoral and evangelization strategy for the parish.

Each of the Small Ministry Groups should reflect on:

- how much they have improved their quality of ministry
- how they have learned and grown in faith together
- their fellowship
- their sense of community
- the number of new disciples they have invited to their group and others
- their sense of communion with the rest of the parish

Between Easter and Pentecost, individual ministry plans can be reviewed and approved against the overall parish strategy for the year ahead. New needs will have been identified, and perhaps there will be an opportunity to form one or two more new Small Ministry Groups. It is also a good time to remind people of the meaning of the Holy Eucharist as our greatest call to mission.

The feast of **Pentecost** should be the great call to action for the year ahead. Family Groups and Small Ministry Groups could be commissioned and re-commissioned. Re-focused and re-energized, work starts to achieve new goals and new objectives.

During **Advent** and **Christmas**, we naturally think of others, and this is a good time to look around our wider community for needs that may give us ideas to improve existing pastoral ministries or to start new Small Ministry Groups. This provides input to the forthcoming review and planning that starts with Lent and is evaluated in the Triduum.

When we approach discipleship as a cycle of growth and development rather than an event, we recognize the true nature of our work. In the process of learning, developing, growing, and supporting each other, our capability for unconditional love continues to increase, and we come closer to the kingdom where we are one with God and each other in Holy Communion.

The important thing is to take the first step and keep going, even if the end result is not certain. On the darkest night, it is only as we take each step that our lamp reveals the path for the next step. With the Light of the World we can step out in confidence.

> Lead, kindly Light, amid the encircling gloom,
>   Lead Thou me on!
> The night is dark, and I am far from home—
>   Lead Thou me on!
> Keep Thou my feet; I do not ask to see
> The distant scene—one step enough for me.
>
> BLESSED JOHN HENRY NEWMAN (1801—1890)

Please continually encourage every member of the parish to pray the prayer of commitment every day and listen to what the Holy Spirit is calling us all to do:

Here I am, Lord. Use me as you will.

BIBLIOGRAPHY

Adams, J.Q. (n.d.). *John Quincy Adams Quotes.* Retrieved July 20, 2011, from Brainy Quotes: http://www.brainyquote.com/quotes/authors/j/john_quincy_adams.html

Agenzia Fides. (2010, 10 20). *Catholic Church Statistics 2010.* Retrieved 06 01, 2011, from Agenzia Fides: http://www.fides.org/aree/news/newsdet.php?idnews=27635&lan=eng

Benedict XVI, P. (2005). *The Yes of Jesus Christ.* Crossroad Publishing.

Benedict XVI, P. (2006, 09 12). *Faith, Reason and the University.* Retrieved 01 03, 2011, from www.vatican.va: http://www.vatican.va/holy_father/benedict_xvi/speeches/2006/september/documents/hf_ben-xvi_spe_20060912_university-regensburg_en.html

Benedict XVI, P. (2009, 05 29). *Benedict XVI's Message to Rome Conference on Laity.* Retrieved 01 02, 2011, from www.zenit.org: http://www.zenit.org/article-26088?l=english

Booker, M. a. (2010). *Evangelism—which way now?* London: Church House Publishing.

Bourg, F.C. (2004). *Where Two or Three are Gathered: Christian Families as Domestic Church.* Indiana: Notre Dame University.

Brennan, P.J. (2007). *The Mission Driven Parish.* New York: Orbis Books, Maryknoll.

Cardinal John Henry Newman. (1801—1890). *The Journey with Jesus—Poems and Prayers—Lead Kindly Light.* Retrieved July 20, 2011, from Journey with Jesus: http://www.journeywithjesus.net/PoemsAndPrayers/John_Henry_Newman.shtml

Catholic Biblical Federation. (2002, 10 28). *Lumko "Seven Step" Method.* Retrieved 02 04, 2011, from Catholic Biblical Federation: http://www.c-b-f.org/start.php?CONTID=11_01_02_00&LANG=en

Chittister, J.D. (2004). *Called to Question*. Plymouth: Sheed and Ward.

Collins, P. (2009). *The Gifts of the Spirit*. Dublin: The Columba Press.

Dulles, A. (1987). *Models of the Church, Expanded Edition*. New York: Doubleday.

Dulles, A. (2002). *Models of the Church, Expanded Edition*. New York: Image Books | Doubleday—Kindle edition.

Fowler, J.W. (2000). *Becoming Adult, Becoming Christian—Adult Development and Christian Faith*. San Francisco: Jossey-Bass.

Gaillardetz, R.R. (2008). *Ecclesiology for a Global Church: A People Called and Sent*. New York: Orbis Books, Maryknoll.

Gaudium at Spes. (1965, December 7). *Pastoral Constitution on the Church in the Modern World Gaudium et Spes Promulgated by His Holiness Pope Paul VI*. Retrieved July 20, 2011, from Vatican: http://www.vatican.va/archive/hist_councils/ii_vatican_council/documents/vat-ii_cons_19651207_gaudium-et-spes_en.html

GDC ©Libreria Editrice Vaticana. (1997, 08 15). *General Directory for Catechesis*. Retrieved 01 03, 2011, from www.vatican.va: http://www.vatican.va/roman_curia/congregations/cclergy/documents/rc_con_ccatheduc_doc_17041998_directory-for-catechesis_en.html

Gravissimum Educationis Vatican II. (1965, 10 28). *Vatican II Declaration on Christian Education*. Retrieved 01 24, 2011, from Vatican: http://www.vatican.va/archive/hist_councils/ii_vatican_council/documents/vat-ii_decl_19651028_gravissimum-educationis_en.html

Jordan, T. (2010, 12 18). *A Nativity Tale*. (P. S. The Daily Telegraph, Interviewer)

Kennedy, J.F. (1962, September 12). *Apollo Program*. Retrieved July 20, 2011, from Wikipedia: http://en.wikipedia.org/wiki/Apollo_program

MacCulloch, D. (2009). *A History of Christianity*. London: Penguin Books Ltd. .

Martineau, Mariette, Joan Weber, and Leif Kehrwald (2008). *Intergenerational Faith Formation: All Ages Learning Together*. New London: Twenty-Third Publications.

Progoff, I. (1975). *At a Journal Workshop*. New York: Dialogue House Library.

Rainer, T.S. (2001). *Surprising Insights from the Unchurched and Proven Ways to Reach Them.* Grand Rapids: Zondervan.

Rolheiser, R. (2006). *Secularity and the Gospel: Being Missionaries to Our Children.* New York: The Crossroad Publishing Company.

Sacrosanctum Concilium. (1963, Dec 4). *Constitution on the Sacred Liturgy Solemnly Promulgated by His Holiness Pope Paul VI.* Retrieved Aug 11, 2011, from Vatican: http://www.vatican.va/archive/hist_councils/ii_vatican_council/documents/vat-ii_const_19631204_sacrosanctum-concilium_en.html

The Passionist Family Group Movement. (n.d.). *Home Page.* Retrieved Jun 08, 2011, from The Passionist Family Group Movement: http://www.pfgm.org/

USCCB. (2005). *National Directory for Catechesis.* Washington: USCCB.

Vatican II—Gaudium et Spes. (1965, 12 07). *Gaudium et Spes.* Retrieved 01 02, 2011, from www.vatican.va: http://www.vatican.va/archive/hist_councils/ii_vatican_council/documents/vat-ii_cons_19651207_gaudium-et-spes_en.html

Vatican II—Lumen Gentium. (1964, 11 21). *Lumen Gentium.* Retrieved 01 02, 2011, from www.vatican.va: http://www.vatican.va/archive/hist_councils/ii_vatican_council/documents/vat-ii_const_19641121_lumen-gentium_en.html

Vehementor Nos. (1906, Feb 11). *Encyclical of Pope Pius X on the French Law of Separation.* Retrieved Aug 15, 2011, from Vatican: http://www.vatican.va/holy_father/pius_x/encyclicals/documents/hf_p-x_enc_11021906_vehementer-nos_en.html

Warren, R. (1995). *The Purpose-Driven Church.* Grand Rapids: Zondervan.

Weldon, M. (2004). *A Struggle for Holy Ground.* Minnesota: Litugical Press, Minnesota.

Westley, D. (1992). *Good Things Happen.* Mystic, CT: Twenty-Third Publications.

Woolley, J. (1984). *I Am With You.* Ropley, Hants: John Hunt Publishing Ltd.

APPENDIX

I. Fowler's Stages of Faith

Here is my own interpretation for our context of Fowler's Stages of Faith from his book *Becoming Adult, Becoming Christian*. I hope that it may help us to look at not just where we are as individuals but also where we are as Church. Perhaps it may help us to gain some understanding of the challenges facing us and encourage us to explore new ways forward. Please note that I am not using Fowler's descriptions of each stage; my comments are an interpretation in the context of my experience, and they are not intended to fully reflect what he meant.

Stage 1

During the first year of life, babies form a give-and-take relationship with those who care for them. In their need and the need of their caregivers to be needed, they both take and give. They learn to trust or distrust, dependent upon the good or bad they experience. Primitive faith takes form from a baby's memories of maternal and paternal presence. Parents go away, but normally they can be trusted to return. In their helplessness babies have their first experience of a greater power over them. They may experience both harshness and nurturing love. These are experiences that later influence their perceptions of God. They experience God in the unconditional love of their parents although they are obviously unaware of the divine significance.

Stage 2

Around age two, children relate more effectively to the world around them. They explore and develop relationships. Life is about novelty and new discoveries. They question everything. Lasting images are formed. Perceptions, feelings, and fantasies play a significant role. Anything seems to be possible. They have few, if any, pre-conceptions. Order and logic will come later.

They form lasting images that hold meaning and wonder. They become aware of death. They begin to differentiate reality from fantasy. Where they are exposed to a religious tradition, the concept of their purpose starts to expand. Symbols and teaching can provide valuable sources of guidance and reassurance, but they can as easily be misused by others to create a permanent influence. Those in this stage develop an awareness of a God who takes on a form based on external influences from parents, family, TV, and stories.

Stage 3

Around the time the child goes to school, they have an understanding of space, time, and cause and effect. Their experiences are much less dependent on feeling and fantasy. Their world becomes more orderly. They take on perspectives from people with whom they have a mutual interest—parents, family, teachers, faith tradition, etc. They recognize that others may have perspectives that are different from their own. They make a distinction between "our people" and others, and this influences inclusion and exclusion. Identity is based on affiliation. The direction and meaning of their life is accepted and is not questioned.

Their approach to right and wrong, good and evil tends to be juridical; goodness is rewarded and badness is punished. Faith is likely to focus on right and wrong, good and evil, with God as the ultimate judge. It seems that God's main preoccupation is with keeping a ledger of our good and bad deeds so that he can reward or punish us according to our behavior. Where the family is part of a religious tradition, faith involves the stories, values, beliefs, and practices of that tradition.

Some people can remain at this stage of faith maturity throughout their lives, especially if fear is a major component of the faith tradition that they belong to. An image of an almighty angry God, just waiting to point out every fault and failing, is a huge disincentive to questioning the authority of your faith tradition. In such a situation people are actively discouraged from questioning, learning, or even thinking about anything other than the answers to the questions formulated by that tradition for their teaching. This is especially common in a repressed society where people lack the knowledge and freedom to question, reflect, and draw their own conclusions.

It is common for many people to remain in this stage of faith throughout their lives. The doctrine and dogma can provide a sense of certainty that is lacking in the world we live in.

Stage 4

In a free society, adolescents begin to assert their independence and idealistically begin to question the values of those around them. Lacking in maturity, they still tend to see things in black and white, right and wrong. They experience a lack of connection between good and reward, and bad and punishment. They see goodness going unrewarded and badness going unpunished. They see the hypocrisy of those in authority and the contradictions between their words and actions. Those they trusted have let them down.

In their doubt they struggle and feel guilt and sadness, especially if their beliefs and values previously provided a sense of certainty and security. If their belief in a juridical God was very certain, the reality that they face in the world may well cause them to doubt the existence of God. As they search for new meaning, people may experiment with the occult, new age spirituality, and a host of others. They may change to another denomination because it is perceived to more accurately live what they preach. There is no lack of idealistic spirituality.

There tends to be a significant drop-off in membership from traditional religion at this stage, and my experience indicates that the Catholic Church is not exempt, despite this being around the time of confirmation for most young people.

People in this stage rely on significant relationships with those they know and trust. They begin to see and understand themselves through others, and they rely on those who have similar values, beliefs, and convictions to form a supportive and orienting unity. In society today, these influences may not always be as positive as they could be. Increasingly, as parents concentrate on their jobs and in the absence of a parish community, they turn to their peers to find the values, beliefs, and convictions to re-orient themselves and find direction.

Where they do find direction in a particular faith tradition, typically there is a clear sense that that tradition has the answers that everyone else is lacking. There is a clear sense of "us" and "the rest" out there. At this stage beliefs are not objectified for critical reflection and inquiry. They are internalized and strongly felt, but they are largely unexamined. Their beliefs are accepted and held dear because they are shared with those they trust.

Most people who remain practicing members of a faith tradition are likely to be at this stage, as most religions tend to promote their exclusiveness and difference from the rest. Within that tradition there is a clear acceptance of those like us and effectively an exclusion of the rest, even while they pay lip service to ecumenism. They emphasize their doctrines and dogma, and outside of permitted boundaries, they actively discourage questioning.

Stage 5

Some people reach a stage where they need to question what their beliefs and values mean because they are often disturbed by the hypocrisy and contradictions found in religion. It is an uncomfortable process.

Initially, there are no apparent answers to the contradictions and hypocrisy. In this emptiness, they may choose literalism, relativism, and disbelief. If something cannot be proven scientifically, it cannot be true. In this mindset, if the Bible is not factually and historically correct, it is just another work of fiction.

As they discover that even science relies on faith that the scientists have objectively explored all the options with full understanding of all the dependencies, they feel less sure of the certainty of science and come to rely only on the truth of their own experience. They choose relativism and exclude the possibility of a universal Truth. "It may be true for you, but not for me." "We are all entitled to our own truth."

This can be very unsettling. People in this stage may struggle to go any further and will stop exploring values and belief in relation to their way of life, in which case they may easily become disillusioned and cynical. Some may make choices and try to live accordingly, but without any critical examination and re-grounding of values and beliefs, at best they achieve a kind of stabilized transitional position.

Is this perhaps where most of those in our secular society are? Have they found traditional religion wanting and are struggling to find answers? Perhaps they have even given up and are just living for the moment? Can we realistically expect people in Stage 5 to accept the Stage 4 approach to faith that they have already rejected?

We are unlikely to find peace and joy in accepting an inadequate belief, which is based only on the evidence of our own experiences. The "truth" that is based on our experience is relative and is continually undermined by the evidence of God—his creation and, most specifically, love. There is a constant challenge that there is much more meaning to our lives than literalism, relativism, and disillusionment.

As a result, some people keep searching for a spiritual connection. They look for it in crystals and New Age movements, tarot cards, the stars, ouija boards, fortunetellers, and in their ancestors. A major criticism of traditional Christian denominations is that they are perceived to lack spirituality.

Stage 6

How do we find God if we cannot see him, hear him, or touch him? We find God in the evidence he has left of his existence in his creation. We all experience God in the love in our relationships. We may not recognize him, but we all long for a pure, accepting, unconditional love. When we experience God in love, he undermines our disbelief, disillusionment, and cynicism. When we realize that love is the action of God in our relationships, we find true spirituality. We find that our soul and the soul of our neighbors around us are inextricably connected to each other through the Holy Spirit of God. It's as if we each have our own well from which we can draw life-giving water, but at the bottom of each well is the same underground lake that is the source of all water and which connects us all together (Progoff, 1975).

In the contradictions between fear and love, fear starts giving way to love. Opposites and contradictions meet and are slowly reconciled. People begin to integrate their contradictory, polarized, or paradoxical experiences. They begin to recognize a God who is both infinitely complex and infinitely simple. They develop a humbling awareness of the power and influence of the spirit in the subconscious, and they come to terms with the reality of who they are. They accept a need to hold opposing tensions together: the conscious and unconscious self; having both a constructive and destructive nature; and perhaps the greatest tension of all, the existence of the kingdom here and now while it is yet to come.

Truth is complex and people in this stage are open to the truths of traditions other than their own. They become aware of the presence of God in all around us. They slowly realize that anyone who loves openly, joyfully, and completely experiences the Way, the Truth, and the Life. They come to realize that Jesus is truly present and known to people even when those people have not yet heard his name or his story. They begin to understand what catholic truly means, and they long for that transforming universality, even as they keep firmly to institutions, commitments, and persons in the present. They recognize the necessity of the tension between the structures of the Church, which often constrain but are necessary to ensure survival, and the universality of the call to discipleship, which challenges us all to go out and follow Christ who has gone before us, even to places and in ways that challenge our understanding of love and acceptance. They take comfort from the fact that the Church recognizes this reality, even while so many continue to seek the security of exclusiveness:

> This Church constituted and organized in the world as a society, subsists in the Catholic Church, which is governed by the successor of Peter and by the Bishops in communion with him, although many elements of sanctification and of truth are found outside of its visible structure. These elements, as gifts belonging to the Church of Christ, are forces impelling toward catholic unity.
>
> *LUMEN GENTIUM,* #8

One word probably best describes people at this stage: tolerance. It is this tolerance that will cause those in earlier stages of faith to doubt that these people are true believers. On the downside, it is also this tolerance that can lock people into inaction at this stage.

Stage 7

People become activists for a truly universal Church based on love. They learn to empty themselves of all the baggage and trappings that hold us back from being love. Material possessions become meaningless. There is no longer any need to have any more than just enough for basic needs. There is real practice of being in communion with God and all of his creation. Having dominion over the earth and all the animals and birds no longer means that they are there for our use, but rather there is deep awareness of the responsibility we have for stewardship for all of God's creation. As activists for the universal Church they embrace not just all of mankind, but all of creation.

> For God who said, "Let light shine out of darkness," has shone in our hearts to bring to light the knowledge of the glory of God on the face of (Jesus) Christ. But we hold this treasure in earthen vessels, that the surpass-

ing power may be of God and not from us. We are af-
flicted in every way, but not constrained; perplexed, but
not driven to despair; persecuted, but not abandoned;
struck down, but not destroyed; always carrying about
in the body the dying of Jesus, so that the life of Jesus
may also be manifested in our body. For we who live
are constantly being given up to death for the sake of
Jesus, so that the life of Jesus may be manifested in our
mortal flesh. So death is at work in us, but life in you.

2 CORINTHIANS 4:6-12

The calm, quiet, and peaceful rejection of the trappings of society, and of any form of personal power of people in this stage,
is very challenging to those around them. Typically their level of
tolerance and acceptance and the level of love that this calls for
is a bridge too far for too many of those around them. These activists are frequently martyred, and then once they are no longer
perceived to be a threat to our current way of life, it is not uncommon to proclaim them saints.

II. Cardinal Avery Dulles' Models of the Church

The Church as Sacrament   (Worship centered round the
sacraments)

Strength: "the Church must in its visible aspects—especially in
its community prayer and worship—be a sign of the continuing
vitality of the grace of Christ and hope of the redemption that he
promises."

Weakness: "the sacramental could lead to a sterile aes-
theticism (devotion to beauty) and to an almost narcissistic
self-contemplation."

Remedy: "As a remedy, attention must be called to the value of structures, community and mission brought out in the other models."

The Church as Herald (Proclaiming)

Strength: [stresses] "the necessity for the faithful to continue to herald the gospel and to move to put their faith in Jesus as Lord and Savior."

Weakness: "the kerygmatic runs the risk of falling into the exaggerations of biblicist and fundamentalist sects. It tends to oversimplify the process of salvation, to advertise 'cheap grace,' to be satisfied with words and professions rather than to insist on deeds, especially in the social and public arena."

Remedy: "As a remedy, one must stress the necessity of incarnating one's faith in life and action."

The Church as Servant (Service)

Strength: "points up the urgency of making the Church contribute to the secular life of man, and of impregnating human society as a whole with the values of the Kingdom of God."

Weakness: "the diaconal could easily give the impression that man's final salvation is to be found within history [simply trying to be better people—in human terms—from generation to generation], and could lure the Church into an uncritical acceptance of secular values, thus muting its distinctive witness to Christ and to its own heritage."

Remedy: "As an antidote, one must insist on the provisional character of any good or evil experienced within history, and on the importance of always looking to Christ and his kingdom."

The Church as Mystical Communion

Strength: "makes it evident that the Church must be united by God by grace, and that in the strength of that grace its members must be lovingly united to one another."

Weakness: "mystical communion, can arouse an unhealthy spirit of enthusiasm; in its search for religious experiences or warm, familial relationships, it could lead to false expectations and impossible demands, considering the vastness of the Church, the many goals for which it must labor, and its remoteness from its eschatological goal."

Remedy: "As a remedy one must call for patience, faith, and a concern for the greater and more universal good."

The Church as Institution

Strength: "makes it clear that the Church must be a structured community and that it must remain the kind of community that God created."

Weakness: "The institutional model, by itself, tends to become rigid, doctrinaire, and conformist; it could easily substitute the official Church for God, and this would be a form of idolatry."

Remedy: "As a remedy the structures of the Church must be seen as subordinate to its communal life and mission."

The Church: A Community of Disciples

Dulles recommended a balance between those models that represented the life and mission of the Church—Sacramental, Herald, Servant, and Community—guided and supported by the Institutional Church.

If we could achieve this we would become a Community of Disciples.

III. Introducing small ministry groups in your parish

Before you start diving in to form Small Ministry Groups, it would be very useful for the parish to understand what they are about and why they are so useful.

Have an off-site retreat day with all parishioners to explore what ideas they have for building up the Church. Make it clear before the meeting that while they may state what they think is not working as well as it could, they should share their ideas on how to solve it—in a constructive positive way. No issue should be left only for "Father" or the parish council to handle.

At the start of the meeting invite the Holy Spirit to lead and guide the discussion by praying: "Here I am, Lord; use me as you will." Re-emphasize that naming problems is not enough; possible solutions should also be offered.

Have a list of all the ministries in the parish, with each one written on a sticky note. Take five flipchart sheets and write one of the five purposes (WORSHIP, WELCOME, WISDOM, WELFARE, and WORD) on the top of each sheet. Explain the importance of the Two Great Commandments and the Great Commission, and then explain the five purposes, emphasizing their interdependence:

- If we receive the Holy Eucharist without also welcoming others, sharing faith together, caring for our neighbor, or proclaiming the good news, we fail to be the sacrament, the outward sign of passing on God's gift of love to us.
- Without ongoing learning and faith sharing, people will have little confidence or enthusiasm for caring for others or proclaiming the good news.
- If we care for others without sharing the good news, we are simply recognized as good people without inviting

others to receive the gifts of God's grace and pass on his love to yet more of creation.

- If we proclaim the good news without the example of caring for others, our actions will not support our words, and few will pay attention.
- If we proclaim the good news but fail to be a welcoming, caring community, people may join, but they will soon leave.

Explain how balancing the work of the parish across all five purposes will lead to becoming a community of disciples, learning and working to live and share a life in Christ. Then stick each note with a name of a ministry onto the sheet whose purpose that ministry promotes. This will illustrate how balanced the work of the parish is across the five purposes and highlight obvious areas of weakness. It should also help to focus the people on talking about specific ministries when they propose ways of overcome existing problems.

Now break the people up into groups of a manageable size, each with a facilitator, to share their ideas of what the problems are and how they might be fixed. Always try to link the problem to a ministry or lack of ministry in the parish, and try to place that ministry within one of the five purposes.

By way of example, when someone says we don't have enough young people attending Mass in the parish, ask what ministries would appeal to young people, who tend to still be energetic, confident, sociable, and idealistic. Explain that being idealistic, if young people can put their faith into action by helping others (Welfare), they will start sharing stories of what their faith means to them with others and start exploring the meaning of their faith (Wisdom). They will also be more inclined to mix socially with people who share those same interests (Welcome) and share those interests with others (Word). Sooner or later on this journey, they will come to appreciate the Holy Eucharist as source and summit of their faith (Worship).

At the plenary session at the end of the day, there are likely to be more ideas than you can deal with, but make sure they are all recorded. Emphasize that this is the start of a journey, not a singular event, and as long as you keep taking one step after the next, you will get there.

Ask for agreement to build up the parish by becoming a Community of Disciples. Confirm that being a disciple does not mean that you have to have great faith or even that you actually have to believe. Remind people that after three years with Jesus, the apostles did not fully believe, and most abandoned him at the Crucifixion. Their faith and courage to act came as a gift of the Holy Spirit at Pentecost. Discipleship is a way of life that involves learning and working to live and share a life in Christ. Emphasize how the five pastoral purposes are the key activities of a Community of Disciples.

Possible next steps may include:

1. Ask existing ministries to explore how the format for small ministry group meetings might be applied to their meetings. At the least, ask them to consider starting the practice of *lectio divina*.

2. Identify any key ministry groups that may be missing, and invite people to volunteer to join them.

3. Ask everyone who is willing to get involved in a ministry of some kind to complete a form listing their gifts and talents and what ministries they are interested in.

4. Agree that the Facilitator's Small Ministry Group will use the ideas and information collected to initiate new small ministry groups.

Before closing, emphasize the importance of ongoing prayer.

IV. Discipleship training for small ministry groups

For good holy order, people need to know what is expected of them. Whenever a new Small Ministry Group is formed (and at frequent periodic intervals for new members), basic discipleship training should be provided within the parish.

The purpose is to ensure that people know how things are done in the parish, what the parish expects of them, and what they can expect from the parish. A consistent way of working reduces the potential for much conflict and stress within a parish, as it creates a focus, improves the effectiveness of work, and ensures fairness by ensuring that rules are not made up as you go along without considering the full implications.

This training is designed to cover key areas of parish life. While the thoughts below are not intended to be comprehensive or complete, they will help you to identify the kind of information that will be useful:

Parish vision and mission

The parish vision and mission is a concise and clear way of explaining what it is trying to achieve, e.g.: "St. Mary's Parish is striving to become a Community of Disciples, worshiping, learning, and working to live and share a life in Christ, centered in the Holy Eucharist as our greatest Call to Mission and Source and Summit of our life and faith."

Disciples will be recognized by their actions to fulfill our mission through the five key pastoral purposes of the Church:

Worship: Prayer and worship together, especially at the Holy Eucharist.

Welcome: Welcoming all and building a community of strong supportive relationships between all members.

Wisdom: Growing in faith and capability for ministry by regularly and actively learning and teaching others, both formally and informally.

Welfare: Engaging in pastoral ministry care for others and serving Christ incarnate in our neighbor.

Word: Consciously and actively inviting people to become disciples of Christ to hear and share the Word of God.

Contemplative Scripture reading (What, Why, and How)

Lectio divina—contemplative reading of the Scriptures is embedded in the recommended structure for Small Ministry Group meetings. It is a great aid to understanding how the Scriptures relate to our lives today as well as being a good vehicle for catechesis.

Catechesis (Why and How)

Many people still think that catechesis is learning the catechism. It is the process whereby people share their faith, their personal experience of Christ, with each other.

Pastoral Ministry (What and Why)

See the relevant chapters in this book.

Evangelization (What and Why)

See the relevant chapters in this book.

Parish organization

- It is useful to explain the difference between a democracy and a theocracy. Clarify the decision-making process.

- People should understand the role of the pastor, especially what he is not expected to do.

Role of the Priest: We often place unrealistic demands on our pastors. Increasingly as more priests have to take on responsibility for more than one parish, it is important to know what can be delegated and what has to be done by the priest. A pastor has four key responsibilities that he has to perform well for an effective, successful parish:

- To administer the sacraments, most especially the Holy Eucharist.
- To preach. He may delegate this responsibility to a deacon.
- To empower, exhort, and support the laity to understand, accept, and carry out their responsibilities to achieve the mission of the Church. This is his key role, as leader and sponsor of change, for the parish to become ever more effective as a Community of Disciples.
- To ensure holy order is maintained in the parish.

These responsibilities do not preclude the pastor from using his particular gifts and talents to participate in or carry out other ministries to build up the Church. However, if his participation in other ministries prevents him from exercising all four key responsibilities above to the best of his ability, there is a grave risk that he will become the single greatest inhibiting factor to the parish becoming a community of disciples.

- The role of the Parish Pastoral Council should be explained.

Role of the Parish Pastoral Council: The key function of the Parish Pastoral Council is to

- Give the priest strategic advice to build up the Church.
- Help to develop the parish vision.
- Put plans in place to achieve the mission to bring about the vision.

The actual work to achieve the vision and maintain the parish should be carried out by appropriate small ministry groups, and the PPC should monitor their effectiveness and progress towards achieving the parish strategy.

- If your parish has Parish Life Coordinators (or a non-ordained Administrator), it will be helpful to explain their role and delegated authority.

Role of Parish Life Coordinators: As pastors are spread ever more thinly, they will have to delegate work to and rely on a few capable and trusted people within the parish. In larger parishes these people are likely to be paid employees of the parish. It is very important that these people not only do a good job but also have an excellent working relationship with the pastor. They will act in accordance with the authority delegated to them by the pastor.

The liturgy coordinator will be responsible for all liturgy small ministry groups to ensure that all liturgy contributes positively to the mission of the Church, in all respects, to a point where the pastor can effectively just show up and preside over great liturgy.

> The pastoral coordinator will be the day-to-day point of contact and decision maker and coordinator for pastoral ministry in the parish, including the small ministry groups with pastoral responsibility.
>
> The administrative coordinator will be the day-to-day point of contact and decision maker and coordinator for administration, finance, and building in the parish, including the small ministry groups with administrative responsibilities.

• Explain the role and responsibilities of the Finance Committee, and especially emphasize their commitment to confidentiality. Include what can be expected in terms of financial reporting.

• Include training on safe environments to ensure the safety and security of children and vulnerable adults.

• Spell out the requirements for progress reporting on the activities of Small Ministry Groups.

Guiding principles
Explain the guiding principles of the parish as discussed in Chapter Seventeen.

Small ministry group roles and responsibilities
Clarify the specific role and responsibilities within each small ministry group and also any small ministry groups whose functions are to support other small ministry groups.

Communication and remaining in communion
Emphasize the importance of good communication on any issue that may affect any other aspect of parish life or any other small ministry group.

Everything about Parish Ministry I Wish I Had Known
KATHY HENDRICKS

This very insightful resource, filled with excellent, wise, and useful tidbits, covers all the practical skills necessary for effective pastoral ministry. It's made richer through Kathy's humorous and hands-on approach.

168 PAGES • $14.95 • 978-1-58595-199-4

Good News Parish Leadership
Trust-Building Guidelines, Tools, and Ideas
MICHAEL L. PAPESH

Author Michael Papesh highlights four essential elements of good news pastoral leadership: ongoing pastoral planning, discernment decision-making, broad and gracious hospitality, and trust building. A fascinating and challenging book for pastoral leaders, associates, pastoral council members, and all who are involved in and committed to parish life.

280 PAGES • $19.95 • 978-1-58595-705-7

Dreams and Visions
Pastoral Planning for Lifelong Faith Formation
BILL HUEBSCH

Here Bill urges parish leaders and ministers to move in the direction of lifelong faith formation by offering parishioners powerful conversion experiences. He also offers a clear and consistent plan for step-by-step growth, with special emphasis on excellent liturgies, strong and effective catechist and teacher formation, and developing households of faith.

160 PAGES • $14.95 • 978-1-58595-638-8

1-800-321-0411
www.23rdpublications.com